shipwrecked

A MEMOIR OF WIDOWED PARENTING AND LIFE AFTER LOSS

JEANETTE KONCIKOWSKI

ISBN: 979-8-35093-559-2 (print)
ISBN: 979-8-35093-560-8 (eBook)

For Grace, Milo, and Brian, whose love carried me to shore and
Mark, whose heart, songs, and stories anchor me still.

TABLE OF CONTENTS

PREFACE

When I first surfaced after my husband died, I found myself in our local bookstore. Ever the bookworm, I had convinced myself that surely there was a handbook that would tell me how my children and I would survive now that life as we knew it had been wrecked. The staff took me to the self-help section where I found memoirs on the hilarious adventures of being widowed. Then I tried the parenting section where I found a picture book full of grieving dinosaurs who could relay the idea of an afterlife to my school-age children. Then the spirituality section, where I found daily meditations on grief, as if I needed help ruminating any harder on what the actual hell we would do now. The book I wanted wasn't there. There was no manual that could help me figure out how to survive this mess my life had become. This solitude and immense loneliness that was already settling into my bones, despite being pretty sure I was still in shock. This BIG oceanic unknown. This place where I was left a widow at only thirty-six; left to parent two grieving and heartbroken children; a place where my own grief, guilt, shame, and anger threatened to consume and overwhelm me to the point of a breakdown. I went home empty-handed.

In the beginning, I was convinced I might drown more often than not in this dark ocean of grief. In the end, I gathered all my strength and got myself and my children to shore. It was no small feat. My body was scarred and bruised along the way. My mind would succumb to the cold. My spirit almost broke. I found myself observing what our experience was like and about two years into our loss, I decided to apply my skills as a researcher and former trauma counselor to write this teaching memoir and its companion workbook. I had a few goals in mind: first, to make sense of what happened to my family; second, to collect the stories and wisdom of other widowed parents; and third, to be that resource on the shelf for someone else in need.

INTRODUCTION

I was looking at the long line of visitors at my husband Mark's wake when I remembered it was Sunday Funday; the one day of the week when my broken family was to be made whole and spend a few hours together and perhaps even have some fun. As I watched my poor, beautiful, brave little girls running through the crowd, new dresses twirling and tights pulled high, I erupted into a fresh stream of tears. Next to me were the remains of their father now encased in marble. I wasn't paying attention to the line of 400 people waiting to talk to me about him. Instead, I mumbled to my husband as if he wasn't in an ash pot now, "How could this be Sunday Funday, Mark? How? How? Goddamn it!"

The next morning, just hours after the Irish wake that had followed the formal wake, I bought tickets to an indoor water park for the following Sunday. In the year preceding his death, Mark and I had often talked about driving the ninety miles to the water park for Sunday Funday. Feeling too unsteady to drive still, nor believing I could handle a full day alone with my children yet, I asked my brother and his son to join us for the trip. It was a quiet drive down that day for the adults, while the kids were giddy in the backseat, wondering where the long mystery ride would end. I was determined that Sunday Funday would continue, even if the "fun" parent was gone. I'd have to be both now; the "heavy rock," as my nine-year-old daughter Grace called me, and the "good-time Dad."

All these years later, my memory of that day has stayed with me. Within ten minutes of arriving, the children were already careening on the slick floor.

"Don't run, G!" I shouted.

"Race you to the top, Mama!" Grace yelled back, barefoot with her swim goggles swinging.

"Don't run at a water park, for the love of all things holy!" I panted, after catching up to her. I grabbed her hand, my other hand already full of five-year-old Veda's fingers, and up the stairs we three climbed to the top of the water slides. Veda and I smooshed into the double inner tube, while Grace readied to race us as a single rider. As we barreled through the twists and turns, the water smacked my cheeks red. Then we plunged under the water. I panicked when I felt for Veda's hand and realized she was not there. I quickly surfaced and found her sitting on top of the tube, peering into the water, looking for me. "Silly Mama, you fell off the tube." I pulled her into me. I breathed. I laughed. I was alive. She was alive. For just a few moments, I forgot why we came to that place. It's possible the girls had forgotten, for almost a whole hour, why we were there. "Let's go!" they shouted, and we ran off to conquer another slide. So began the days, weeks, months, and years of figuring out how to parent through widowhood.

To me, this small snapshot in time of my family at the water park, broken and bereft while simultaneously finding joy in our shared laughter, in our touch, in our time together that felt so bittersweet, would become the epitome of resilient parenting through widowhood. I felt like we were survivors of a shipwreck who had gone overboard. Searching for each other, grabbing onto whatever was floating by to create moments of connection and joy, all the while the larger questions and abyss of *what now* and *what's next* swirled around us in the fast-moving water.

The grief came in waves. I'd cry until I literally couldn't force my body to make more tears in one sitting. There was a dark abyss within my grieving, as deep as the sea, that seemed to hold me down and was unrelenting. That first year, time often felt like it was standing still. Months after my husband's death felt like decades since I had held him. Then, just when I was sure I was going to drown in the ocean of tears that had come once again, a ripple of light on the surface beckoned. Just like the plunge at the end of the waterslide, I surfaced. I breathed. I began again. I swam to shore, with my children in tow.

In this teaching memoir, I share the story of my family—our scars and our strengths. I've also included the lessons I've learned along the way at the end of most chapters. These practical tips and strategies are written with the intention to help pull you from wave to wave until you make it to shore, and rebuild your life after loss. You can also read the stories from the widowed parents I've interviewed and learn more from experts in the field of grief by reading the companion workbook to this memoir, *Stronger Than The Storm: A Guidebook for Widowed Parents on Surviving and Thriving After Loss*. The workbook includes assessments, worksheets, and even more practical advice to help you process your own loss experience, needs, and desires for your life in the "after."

I want you to know that the "after" does not have to be tragic, even though it will often feel that way. Losing your spouse and caring for yourself and your children through your grief will likely be the hardest thing you will ever go through. Trust yourself. Trust the process. Trust other people to help you because you cannot do this alone. Grieve your person and grieve hard. Surrender to your pain, because it is only in knowing your pain, holding it, letting it come in wails, fits, and sobs that it will break you open and be released. You will not die from your grief, even though some days you think you might. Your voyage will not be easy. It will take its toll on you and your kids. It will shake you to your core. But, if you let it, it will transform you all so that you can move forward into your new life with peace; a life where your loss becomes a tender place, a soft patch of ocean-kissed sand, where you and your beloved will always live. It is in this place where you can find the strength and sense of calm you need to begin again.

Peace to you and your children,
Jeanette

PART I

Drowning

ONE

Before We Entered the Eye of the Storm

We three girls giggled as we clamored for the phone, each trying to take it away from the other and talk to the DJ. From the kitchen, our friend shouted, "You're on! You're on the air!"

"This one goes out to Sean, Mark, and Jason from Jeanette, Lisa, and Tasha," boomed the DJ in his rich baritone. We hung up the phone and sang along to Mariah Carey's high-pitched track, *Emotion*, wondering the rest of the night whether there was any likelihood that three teenage boys would be listening to the adult slow-jam station that Friday night in the summer of 1993. It was the first night Mark Koncikowski entered my consciousness.

My childhood best friend, Lisa, was the one with the crush on mystery Mark. A month after calling the radio station, I was sitting in Spanish class on the first day of our sophomore year when the boy sitting next to me said, "Me llamo Mark Koncikowski," as the Señora made her way through roll call. I stole glances at him for the next thirty-four minutes, wondering what my shy friend saw in him. I could tell by the way he moved, by the way he mocked the teacher, by the way he looked at me, that he was going to be trouble. A few hours later, he strolled past Lisa and me on the bus. To our credit, we pretended not to pay attention. A few days later, Lisa grew tired of my insistence that she should just tell Mark how she felt, so I offered to scope out the situation for her. I boldly plopped myself down in the seat next to him on the bus and asked if he had a girlfriend. A slow smile came over his curled lip. "Nah," he said, "Not yet." His hazel eyes, with lashes longer than my own, held my stare. I hurriedly wrote a phone number on the palm of his hand, telling him to call me on the house phone where I was babysitting that night.

Three hours later, we were alone on the phone. Turned out we liked the same music, planned to have careers as writers in the big city someday, and we held the same disdain for the Catholic Church that we, and every other kid from South Buffalo, had been born into. Before I had to return home, I mentioned that I had an ulterior motive to the call and wanted to know if he, perhaps, liked Lisa. Mark grew quiet for the first time since we started talking. "Um, that's too bad you asked that, because I do like someone, but it's not your friend." And the rest, as they say, is history.

In true fifteen-year-old fashion, we secretly dated for ten days before we broke up. He told me he "couldn't handle the commitment" when I told him I couldn't keep lying to my friend if this thing was going to be forever. For years, Mark and I debated which one of us caused the big break-up. It lasted two-and-a-half months. To make him suffer, I went out with a football jock and publicly flirted with another ex-boyfriend. I made him wait another month. We began dating again on December 2nd, 1993. We were together for the next twenty-one years.

I will do my best to sum up those years for the sake of brevity. But how can you succinctly relay the kind of relationship that brings you to your knees? That stirs something inside of you that tells you have met your mirror; the one who reflects all your parts back to you? No one will ever understand me the way Mark did nor could anyone else possibly understand his complexities like I did. Even after his last breath, the potent connection I felt with Mark has never stopped.

From the start, Mark and I had an intense relationship. Somewhere amongst the stolen kisses and hurried touching in new adolescent love, I described to him the terrible traumas I had experienced as a child, at the hands of a family member. At fifteen years old, Mark did for me what none of the adults in my life were able to do: he validated my experiences, he listened with compassion, and he told me what happened to me wasn't my fault. He vowed to protect me.

Over and over again, Mark would come to my rescue in the years that followed. Yet Mark wasn't without a dark side of his own. Somewhere in the second year of our relationship, like many other alienated teens in the 1990s, this clean-cut schoolboy transformed into an angry goth kid, complete with a heavy air of depression that seemingly came out of nowhere. It was in our senior year, shortly after we both received news that we had gotten into a prestigious private college (and for which I had received a full scholarship), that Mark tried to kill himself. His parents admitted him to the local psychiatric hospital and told me he would be going to one of the local colleges after graduation. His suicide attempt terrified me. I couldn't imagine my life without him, so I opted to stay at home for undergrad as well.

A string of mental health diagnoses followed Mark after that first and only trip to the psychiatric hospital: bipolar disorder, schizoaffective disorder, major depression with hypomania. As we moved through our early adulthood together, I became convinced that at some point he would break again. My anxiety haunted me, and I worried about what would happen to me if something happened to Mark.

Good things and terrible things happened in that first decade of adulthood. Mark's mother died suddenly of a heart attack when we were 19, just a little over a year after his suicide attempt. I credit his mentor in college with saving his life in his grief. He gave him a pen to put to paper and encouraged him to write his way out of the darkness. Writing poetry provided Mark a chance to exhale, at least some of the time. His dark days would still come, but I grew better at anticipating them. Sometimes I knew when to leave him alone. Sometimes I knew when to sit outside his house, waiting in my car, in case he decided he needed me. I had no idea how unhealthy this dynamic was. There were a few blow-up fights where I'd threaten to leave him, but he'd always promise to change. My own anxiety was ever present and the thought of being alone and vulnerable in the world without his protection and care stopped me. I thought about seeing other people, though. I even went so far as to apply to graduate school in Boston, Ann Arbor, and Berkley. Then, when a letter from

Harvard actually arrived, offering me a spot in their Graduate School of Education program, I gave Mark an ultimatum. Get it together enough to come to Boston with me or let me go. I wasn't giving up Harvard, which I saw as the means to my permanent escape from a troubled childhood. Mark's response was to plan a romantic trip away for my birthday, during which he proposed to me. I, of course, said yes.

When we returned home at the end of our weekend, my mother was waiting for us. I had expected her to cry happy tears over the news of our engagement, and she did, in a way that seemed excessive. She then informed us that she had just learned she had breast cancer and it was serious. I told her I would write to Harvard and postpone admission for a year. My mother insisted that I go. Despite the regular conflicts I had with my mother in my teenage years, I knew she was proud of me. I was the first in our family to go to college— and I had been accepted into the most prestigious university in the world for graduate school. So, that summer, while my mother was undergoing chemotherapy, Mark and I packed up a U-Haul and headed out for a new beginning in Boston.

I savored one of the best years of my life in Boston, enjoying the new surroundings, the intellectual rigor of Harvard, and the new friendships I made with other students. The only job Mark could get was working at a group home an hour outside of the city and it required him to take two buses and then the subway nightly. He worked the late shift from four in the afternoon until midnight. He'd arrive home and crash. A few hours later, I'd head out for my own buses and subway commute shortly after dawn. We didn't see much of each other during the week. When his depression lessened, we'd spend the weekends exploring our new city. After I graduated from Harvard, we decided to stay near Boston, as my mother was in remission, I had a good job offer, and Mark had finally found his place working at a school for adults with developmental disabilities. Another year went by, and the school administrators he worked for asked us to consider starting a nonprofit to manage the group home they were opening for their adult students to live year-round. We jumped at the chance to do something meaningful, and the project gave Mark a sense of responsibility. He flourished that year and threw himself into his work to help turn a foreclosed house into the group home. But a few months after the renovations were completed, it all came crashing down. The school administrators (who were longtime community activists but not business-minded people) lost a major grant and suddenly couldn't pay Mark's salary. With our financial stability seemingly vanishing overnight, we decided to return to our hometown of Buffalo, just six weeks before our wedding.

I remember shaking off the little voice in the back of my head that asked me if I was really ready to commit to a lifetime of care for Mark, given his depression. I truly believed I owed him my own life. As we said our vows on a hot September day in 2002, I told that voice to quiet down and not come back. And then, like so many women before me, I thought the logical next step in sanctifying our union would be to have a baby. Nature did not agree. I struggled through the next two years with infertility. Mark, who had seemed rather non-chalant to my enthusiasm for a baby during all of our baby-making efforts, was absolutely ecstatic when it finally happened.

My pregnancy was difficult. I was on bedrest due to bleeding for most of my pregnancy. We had three separate incidents where we were told we had miscarried the baby, only for a doctor to later find a heartbeat. Our daughter, Grace, was born via emergency c-section at 32 weeks in April 2005. After passing out at the end of the surgery, I came to and asked for my baby and my husband. The nurse said, "Don't worry, dear. Your husband hasn't left that baby's side since the minute she was born. He said to tell you that you are the bravest person he's ever met, and you'll be fine. Your little girl needs him right now."

By the time I was allowed to meet Grace in the neonatal intensive care unit (NICU), Mark had already held her, changed her, bathed her, fed her a bottle, and tucked her back into her incubator. The six weeks Grace spent in the NICU were the best six weeks in our relationship. We functioned like a perfect team, in lock step with each decision as we learned to care for her and make heavy decisions together. It seemed becoming a father might change Mark's makeup after all, as surely as becoming a mother would change mine. One of the happiest days of our married lives was the day we brought Grace home.

A year after Grace was born, Mark entered graduate school with the goal of becoming a chiropractor. Between his love for me and the baby, his busyness with school and a part-time job, it seemed his depression was (mostly) well controlled for his first two years in the doctorate program. As the demands of his training grew in the third year, though, Mark's depression came back. It seemed worse than ever before, and he was regularly having suicidal ideation. He refused to see a therapist to help him cope with it. It was only when I cried and pleaded or threatened to leave that he'd finally go and talk to a professional about it. He'd see a therapist for one or two sessions and then not go back again. We rinsed and repeated that cycle for another year, including while my mother, rather unbelievably, went through a second type of breast cancer (not a recurrence of the first). This time she had to suffer through a double mastectomy, radiation, and more chemotherapy. When things seemed better for both her and Mark, Mark and I decided it was the right time to grow our family again. I conceived right away the second time around and, much to our relief, baby Veda was born in March 2009, following a completely normal pregnancy and natural birth. Mark worked part-time and continued his studies after Veda's birth. I don't know if his depression lessened during this time or if I just stopped giving it so much of my attention now that two children needed me, but it no longer dominated our family landscape in the way it had before.

When Mark's dark spells did come, I believed it best for his sake, and for mine, to keep his depression private. We never spoke about it with anyone other than one or two of our closest friends. Publicly, we always seemed happy together. I still believed that I could love him to better mental health.

Then, in 2010, I found myself unexpectedly pregnant again, even though I was still nursing Veda. I felt great ambivalence about this pregnancy and even considered a termination. I couldn't fathom how I could handle taking care of one more person. Mark assured me he would help more, but he was entering his residency year in chiropractic school, which required that he see patients in clinical practice in addition to his full load of classes and part-time job. As with my earlier pregnancies, I had horrible morning sickness and struggled to function. A week after we told our families about the pregnancy, we went in for a sonogram. I remember vividly a fight we had in the parking lot about juggling all of these responsibilities and how my ambivalence came roaring back in, like a tightness bearing down on my chest. But then we went inside and I got all gooped up; there on the screen was our perfect fourteen-week-old little bean—now with arms and legs. In an instant, all of my doubts disappeared, and I kissed Mark with a heart full of joy. Thirty seconds later, that joy drained out of my face as I watched the technician hurriedly leave the room to get a doctor. Then the doctor frowned while looking at the screen and left the room. When she came back, she had my midwife on the phone. They told us that the fetal heartbeat, which had been strong at the initial ultrasound seven weeks ago, was gone. They believed the baby had died sometime in the two preceding weeks. The only day they could arrange a D&C for me, since my body had not let go of the baby on its own, was on our eighth wedding anniversary. Two weeks after it was over, I held a tiny box with a tiny amount of ashes in it. One month later, on the morning of Halloween's eve we buried the baby's ashes in our garden. Mark wrote a beautiful poem for him (I believed the baby was a boy) and that was the last Mark ever acknowledged our loss.

The ambivalence I carried about the pregnancy quickly transformed into guilt, which was compounded by grief. For the first time in my life I felt true depression. Mark and I drifted further away from each other, as fall turned into winter and winter into spring. Mark's depression also worsened during this time. Sometimes he would explode with anger towards me; sometimes he would sit in a chair, staring into space for hours. He refused all of my attempts to get him help. I still did not tell anyone what he/we were going through. I did my best to protect Grace and Veda from noticing our angst. Like my mother had taught me, image was everything. *It was fine. It would all be fine,* I whispered to myself.

Just as my depressive fog started to lift in the new year of 2011, my mother became sick again. The first cancer had returned, spreading to her spine and liver. I spent the next year and a half caring for her. Mark finished school and opened his own chiropractic practice. Business was slow, so he took part-time work back at the group home where he had worked on and off since we had returned from Boston. He enjoyed working with both client populations and this seemed to stabilize him. He sounded hopeful about the future for the first time in a long time.

Something happens when you feel life getting topsy-turvy. As Mark seemed to steady and my mother slipped away from the world, I found myself reevaluating all of my life choices. I realized how very unhappy I was in our marriage, and I started thinking a separation would help me sort out my feelings. Unlike all the other times I had talked myself out of it (mostly for the sake of the children), this time I started saving money, just in case. I found a new therapist who asked me questions that suggested our marriage was, in fact, wholly unhealthy.

As I went through the motions that spring, Mark went on a health kick, even agreeing to try a new antidepressant with hopes of finally keeping his depression permanently at bay. By May 2012, it was apparent my mother wouldn't have much time left. Mark tried to help me manage my anxiety about her pending death by doing yoga together regularly. One afternoon, Grace, Mark, and I were all in triangle pose and the next minute, he was unconscious on the living room floor. When he came to, he chalked it up to not eating a hearty enough breakfast.

A few days later, as we made lunch for the kids, Mark opened the refrigerator door to retrieve the milk. As we chatted, I watched his hand with the milk in it start to tremor, then tremble, and then he dropped the milk. Almost instantly, Mark also dropped to the floor. This time, he hit his head and seemed confused upon regaining consciousness. He refused to go to the hospital and I think I was so averse to the idea of more bad news in our lives, I let it go. Denial had become my companion. Another week or so went by and one day I found him staring absently into space. I was unable to get his attention. I had to physically shake him to get him to respond. This time I insisted he see a doctor. He refused. After a few more incidents like these, he finally agreed. His doctor then wanted him to see a neurologist, who wanted to run some tests, including an EEG. My father and I were caring for my mother around the clock by that point, so I didn't go with him for any of the tests.

If there was a blessing in my mother's death in July 2012, it was that she and I made our peace and that she died at home with her family by her side. Before that first week without her was over, we were to receive more bad news. The neurologist called with a request for Mark and me to both come in to discuss the results of his tests as they believed he had epilepsy. I remember thinking then, *how much worse can life get?*

At the appointment, the doctor explained to us that not all seizures are grand mal (also known as tonic-clonic) seizures, which are often the type of seizures people associate with convulsions and epilepsy. Mark was experiencing absent seizures (when he stared off into space) and drop seizures (when he lost consciousness). The doctor said tests showed his epilepsy was occurring in his temporal lobe, the emotional center of the brain. He speculated that Mark's mental health issues were a result of lifelong, undiagnosed epilepsy. This explained why Mark had heard voices in his head when he was a child, as sometimes people having a seizure hear voices before or after the seizure, as well as the trance-like states he'd go into when playing video games. It explained his intractable depression that had never responded to any medication or therapy and it explained what was happening to him now. His diagnosis revealed why Mark had not once, not twice, but three times in our adult life had accidents in which he fell down stairs, fell in the shower, or lost consciousness. The doctor feared the seizures were increasing enough for there to now be a pattern and be visible to others and thought perhaps the new antidepressant had lowered his threshold for them. He said Mark needed to stop the antidepressant and be put on medication to control the seizures immediately. He also told us that New York State law did not allow people with uncontrolled epilepsy to drive. Mark would have to surrender his license.

We were shocked. Mark was devastated by the news, especially with losing his driver's license, which he viewed as losing his independence, and with having to stop the antidepressant and start on an antipsychotic drug (as most drugs that are anticonvulsants are categorized as such). As the news settled, I actually felt relief. There was a biological reason, centered in his brain as to why Mark behaved the way he did. Why one minute he could be full of life and laughter, and then, with the flip of an invisible switch, sit near catatonic for hours in a chair. I thought at the time that this explained our explosive fights and our mutual unhappiness. I asked myself what kind of person would leave their spouse when they were newly diagnosed with a chronic illness? Especially when the person wasn't liable for their behavior because of a malfunction with the electrical signals in their brain? *For better or worse, in sickness and in health*, played over in my head. I resolved to stay.

Within a few weeks, I had gone from managing my mother's medication needs to managing Mark's, as he had serious side effects, and it was difficult to convince him to take the medication as it seemingly was doing little to stop the seizures. In fact, it seemed to worsen them. Mark had seizures when he was alone at his office and even had one in front of a patient. Within three months, it became clear he could not continue to practice independently as a chiropractor. Nine months after we opened his chiropractic business, we were forced to close it. For the next year, we struggled mightily. Mark got a job as an assistant chiropractor but it was an hour away from our home. I drove him back and forth for months, despite also trying to hold down my own job and care for the children largely alone. Our marriage was crumbling and, this time, everyone could see it. The silver lining was that Mark's seizures finally started to stabilize that summer of 2013.

And then another shoe dropped. Mark, the children, and I were just leaving the county fair that August when I received a call from a long-time friend. His wife, Sofia, who had been my closest girlfriend since I was eighteen, had suffered a massive heart attack that morning. My relationship with Sofia over the last few years had been punctuated with periods of tension and estrangement, but still, I loved her like a sister and was devastated by the news. I demanded to know what hospital she was at and told him I was on my way. Then, he uttered the words in a tone so soft I could barely make them out: "She's gone." I threw the phone across the parking lot in my shock and despair. Sofia had died at the age thirty-seven, leaving behind her husband and young children.

A few days later, I approached Sofia's casket on the arm of her brother. Peering in and seeing someone my own age that I loved lying there became more than I could bear. I left the wake seething that Mark had refused to take time off to attend her services with me. The next day, full of anger and guilt, I shook with sobs in my car while trying to muster up the courage to walk into her funeral. Sofia's death finally opened the floodgates to the grief of my mother's death. In my relationship with each of them, I had done and said things I was not proud of, even though I loved both of them deeply. Unlike my mother, I didn't get to reconcile those feelings with Sofia. I couldn't remember what our last conversation was but I hope it ended with her requisite, "Love ya!" All I wanted was for my husband to comfort me in my sorrow, but he was not there. My anxiety became so overwhelming that I ran into the church, headed straight for the bathroom, and threw up. Coming home that day after her funeral, I knew I was done with my marriage to Mark. I hardly spoke to him for the next three weeks as I came in and out of my own darkness. During that time, he got his driver's license back and I made my plan to leave. I had not planned to end my marriage on its 11th anniversary, but by the time the day was over there was no other choice. After an explosive day together and a night that is still too difficult to put into written word, I packed Mark a bag and asked him to leave.

Every day in those early weeks of our separation, Mark implored me to take him back with promises of change. I held to my mantra, "I love you unconditionally. I always will. But our marriage has conditions. And until those conditions are met, we cannot be together." Separating our lives was no easy feat. I involved lawyers and counselors and his doctors. I wanted to ensure we all were safe and as cared for as possible. I needed to know our children would be safe in his presence and he would be safe from his epilepsy. I desperately tried to control it all.

When a marriage is on the rocks, you can't help but start to wonder what YOU need to be doing in life to be more satisfied. Alice, my therapist at the time, asked, "What if, instead of seeing this as a time of only grief and loss, you also see this as a time to reclaim you? What is it that you've always wanted to do, Jeanette, but never did? Make a list."

As I pondered her question, it occurred to me that I had never really considered what I wanted in my future beyond a break from Mark. I made a list, and it had things "all-controlling Jeanette" thought were ridiculous, like horseback riding and boxing lessons. I told myself to just try something on the list. By the end of the following week, I was sitting on a horse, led around an arena by Beth, the horseback riding instructor I had just hired. It thrilled me.

Every Friday night thereafter, I'd go straight from work to Beth's farm. I had never gotten on a horse until I was thirty-six years old, but here I was, horse crazy. Walking, and then later riding Barnaby, a beautiful brown Clydesdale, around the arena, something akin to happiness started to swell. Week after week, I learned new skills, thanks to Beth's calm and steady approach to teaching. The Jeanette who had always been so fearful and so anxious was suddenly riding at fast speeds on a one-ton animal that would crush her if we went down together. I reveled. Barnaby and my Fridays (and then Saturdays at the farm) gave me a new life; a life within and outside of myself that I didn't know I was missing. I felt a growing competence. I felt joy. Cruising around on Barnaby, I felt free. At the end of each lesson I'd put away his tack and coax him back into this stable with an apple. I'd never felt such an intense connection with an animal before. He'd look at me with his big brown eyes and it was like he was saying, *"You are okay. You're not alone. We can get through this together."*

Over the next few months, I rebuilt myself and my self-esteem. Mark, however, could only seem to hold himself together when he was with the girls. On his days off from parenting, he spiraled. He quit the assistant chiropractic job. He bounced from friend's couch to friend's couch, partying hard with nothing to do to fill his time until he would clean up for his days with the girls. It was hard on us all. When Mark and I saw each other, we would argue more than not. My resentment at the years I lost "managing" him couldn't help but spill out whenever we were together. I couldn't break from him completely. Three months after separating, I let him back into my bed. It was Christmas Eve, after all, I rationalized.

Our relationship ebbed and flowed for another eight months. Even though I struggled to disentangle sexually and emotionally from Mark, I felt it of utmost importance to separate financially, especially since he seemed to be digging deeper and deeper into debt. Mark was furious at my decision to move forward with a formal separation agreement. I became equally enraged when my lawyer informed me that as part of the agreement, I would have to pay Mark alimony as I was the higher income earner in the marriage, and he hadn't worked steadily in the last five years. That's when I started boxing lessons. One morning a week. I'd work out my anger on the bag and on the cute trainer I had hired to teach me how to box. Boxing, like riding, provided a connection to my body and to my power in a new and exciting way.

Everything with Mark during this time was a negotiation. The only way he agreed to the legal separation was on the condition that I would go on a date with him once a month. I resented him for this non-legally binding requirement, but I held up my end of the agreement. I knew signing the papers to separate broke his heart. If we coexisted peacefully for a year with the arrangements we had, I could ask the judge for a simple divorce decree, and it would be over. Once it was determined that we would continue joint custody of our girls, I had to accept that my anger was getting in the way of them being okay. The girls didn't understand why our family was hurting and both were angry with me since it was clear to them, and Mark, that I was the "bad guy" who was disrupting our family unit. When they were with Mark, it was like a great big limitless sleepover. They slept in until noon and then stayed up all hours, watching movies and cartoons together in the middle of the night. Mark would make s'mores for breakfast. Then the girls would come back to me, and I'd try to restructure their lives. They took all of the changes in stride but almost a year into shuffling between the two of us, it was clear that our separation was taking its toll on them, too. My vivacious children were brooding more than not.

With the help of a family therapist, Mark and I decided that we would spend every Sunday together as a family, which would be the one day a week we'd try to put our angst aside to function as a whole for them. This is how Sunday Funday began. Thankful for the blessing that their young ages afforded us in the girls not fully understanding what was happening in our adult relationship, we both put on masks for their sake. Despite the difficulties in our relationship, Mark did his best to be a good father. He could pull himself together in front of the children in a way he could never do with me. He loved them in all the ways he longed to be loved as a child, often acting more as a playmate than a parent. Every Sunday, from that point on, he'd come over and the four of us would have breakfast together, then plan a fun trip or activity for the afternoon and come home and cook dinner together. Then Mark would head back out to wherever he went when he wasn't with us.

Mark still insisted he and I have a date once a month, convinced he could convince me to ease off this separation. After two months of date days with Mark, during which I refused to speak to him, I planned the third month's date, wanting to show Mark how I had changed. He had no idea we were going on a wintry horseback ride at a nearby dude ranch. I kept my business-like approach to the whole thing until I saw Mark struggle to mount the horse after watching me skillfully climb aboard. It was his first time riding a horse and his first time seeing me ride. I couldn't help but laugh as he struggled throughout the ride to keep control of his horse. At one point, his horse refused to move, no matter how he pleaded and prodded. The guide and I circled back to see what was the issue. Mark was imploring the horse to go up the hill, but the horse just stood there and then it let out a massive burst of gas and we erupted into laughter. We laughed until we cried, as the horse galloped up the hill with Mark barely holding on. The instructor snapped a picture of us before we ended the ride. There is a distance between us, but we are both grinning and our eyes are glistening from our laughter. We stopped for coffee on the way home and sat around a firepit, outside the cafe. As I plopped my muddy boots up on the bricks and talked to him about my love of riding, he looked at me endearingly and said with sadness in his voice, "I don't know who you are anymore, Jenny."

"I think I'm becoming the me I was meant to be," I replied softly. We had a quiet ride home.

Our date days and Sunday Fundays were less contentious after that. Eventually, I even started to look forward to them. I started to relax into this new phase of our life. Around April or May of 2014, things started looking up for Mark too. He returned to work as a counselor at a smoking cessation hotline, a job he held while in chiropractic school. I was shocked when he told me that he had started therapy and that it was going well. As spring shifted into summer, I agreed to resume marriage counseling. Between bi-monthly marriage counseling sessions, Sunday Fundays, and date days, we were seeing each other more and more. The deep connection we had at earlier points in our relationship started to rekindle. We'd still fight, but it was starting to lessen as the marriage counselor illustrated the unhealthy patterns we had locked into our relationship. I read a lot on co-dependency and could see the ways I had expected Mark to take care of me and how I had felt unsafe in the world without him guiding me through it. The marriage counselor made a contract with Mark that he would be the one, not me, who Mark would call when in crisis or if experiencing suicidal thoughts again. I doubted Mark would stay true to his word, but sure enough, when Mark's dark days came upon him, he called the counselor instead of me. I was flabbergasted. It felt freeing to not have to worry about him. I think during that time I also made my peace with the fact that it wasn't my responsibility, but Mark's, to keep him safe, healthy, and alive.

Though I was still irritated that I had to underwrite Mark's life financially, we were each forced to grow in new ways. Mark picked running back up as a way to help him cope and to get fit. I'd see him run by the house some mornings when I sat on the porch having my coffee. He'd wave to me as if a neighbor and I'd watch him go, equal parts proud of him for getting himself so together and sad that it took so long to happen.

In July of that year, Mark, who had been living with his father at that point, told me that he wanted to move out of his father's house. He looked at me as if waiting for me to invite him home. I told him I wasn't ready to move back in together, but I would help him look for an apartment nearby—an apartment I knew my alimony payments would cover. The girls and I helped Mark move into an apartment a few blocks away in mid-August. The apartment was just behind their school. We could walk between his apartment and our home, passing their school midway. Mark wouldn't need to drive the girls anywhere to meet their needs. It was an ideal situation and we hoped the girls would start to feel more stable. We even took a family vacation together the week after he moved out. I still felt confused about the ultimate fate of our marriage, but I told myself to stay in the present moment and not fast forward to any next steps.

For the rest of that summer into the early fall of 2014, we were seeing each other three or four nights a week; one of us sneaking back to the other's place after the kids went to bed, making sure they didn't awaken to see us together, as we didn't want to further confuse them. For our 12th wedding anniversary, a year from the episode that led to my making him leave, we went to an adventure park and spent the day climbing through trees on a ropes course. Mark took a video on his phone of me just before I had to zip line down the final run. In it, you can see me, nervous on the treetop plank. "I can't do it, Mark. I'm too scared."

He replies, "I love you. You've got this. Just jump."

I jumped and screamed in joy and terror the whole way down. In the souvenir picture we purchased that day, we are smiling with our arms around each other. I couldn't believe how much had changed in a year and realized I didn't regret leaving. Whether I would stay or go forward with the divorce, I felt that both Mark and I were healing and that whatever happened, we'd be better parents, friends, and people for it.

Mark was diligent with his counseling and medical appointments. As far as I knew, he was seizure-free and taking his medication. By early October, my thoughts turned to Christmas and also to the fact that in February, it would be one year since our formal separation and I could decide whether to ask the court for a divorce. While I didn't *have* to make a decision about the divorce, it started gnawing at me. I felt hopeful our marriage was in the process of deep healing, but I was also afraid to give up this newfound freedom. I really liked the person I was becoming, and I worried that if we moved back in together, we would slip quickly back into our old patterns. I concluded that it would help for Mark and me to have some dedicated time alone. As our last Christmas had been so difficult, I wanted to make up for it.

But first, there was the matter of what to do about his sister's wedding. Mark's older sister had recently been married in the Caribbean and was now to have a reception back at home. Mark asked me to attend it with him and the girls. I hadn't seen his family much since we separated and worried about how they would react to me being there. For our October date, we went shopping for clothes to wear to the reception. Mark had never really concerned himself with what I wore, but as I looked through the racks, he came up behind me and whispered in my ear that it would be sexy if he picked out what I wore. I laughed at the idea but let him pick out two dresses for me that I thought were too tight to wear to a family wedding. He came into the dressing room with me, kissing my neck as I changed and telling me he couldn't wait to get me home. I brought both dresses home with me and wore one to the wedding reception. Despite my concerns, we had a great time that night. Dancing together, the girls twirling next to us, I felt like we had come full circle. I held him close as we danced and didn't hide my feelings for him in front of his family. We kissed and I snuggled into him, telling him how much I loved him. The photographer took a picture of the four of us together, all smiles. An intact family. A happy family. As he lay beside me sleeping that night, I went online and booked a post-Christmas getaway, just for the two of us. It would be the first time in years we'd have more than one overnight away from the kids. After thirteen months of separation, I wanted to see if we could manage four days alone. This would be my Christmas gift to him. If all went well, I would tell him on the trip that I wasn't going to file for divorce. I never got the chance.

TWO

Shipwrecked

As I dressed for work the morning of Thursday, October 30th, 2014, I didn't know that two hours later, I'd be hysterical and tearing at the same blazer I was now taking care to iron. I was supposed to be giving a big presentation that morning, which could net me a long-sought promotion. Mark was late to pick up our girls and take them to school. He agreed to come at 7:30 a.m. so I could get to the office early to set up. It was now 7:35 and he was not answering his phone. I packed the girls into the car.

I replayed the events of the night before, as I drove the quick two blocks to Mark's apartment. He had called to tell me he had three seizures at the start of his shift at work that evening. "You shouldn't be alone if you are having them again. Come home tonight," I said.

"I'm fine," he replied, "I told you I can handle it."

"Have you been taking your meds, Mark?"

"Stop treating me like a child, Jeanette," he growled. Then, he said a little more softly, "Of course I have, Jen."

Around 10:30 p.m., he called to say he was safely in his apartment. I told him I loved him, and he should call me at any point if he needed me. He said it was time he learned how to take care of himself when sick.

These were the first seizures I was aware he was having in thirteen months. Like other people with epilepsy, when Mark had seizures, he would sleep for hours afterwards. It was not uncommon for him to sleep twelve or more hours at a time. I assumed this was what had happened and why he hadn't shown up that morning. I was equal parts angry and worried. Angry that he refused to get a roommate or live with a family member who could keep an eye out for his safety and worried that he still wasn't answering the door. Angry that he never followed through on giving me a key to his apartment, even though our relationship seemed to be in recovery mode.

When I pulled into the parking lot that morning, Mark's car was in its assigned spot. I ran up the stairs with Veda in my arms and Grace clinging to my hand, trying to keep pace with my frenzy. Banging on the door, I thought I could rouse him. I waited for him to answer, either sleepily or angrily, just as he had done two weeks before when he hadn't answered his phone and I rushed over to make sure he was okay.

"I'm fine! Stop being neurotic!" he yelled at me then. "If you want me to be more independent, then let me be independent!" he exclaimed, slamming the door in my face. But on this day, there was no answer at his door. My frenzy turned into a panic.

"Mark! Open the door, Mark!" I had never met his neighbors, but I banged on their door. After I explained my concern, his neighbor invited me in, and I left the girls in the home of this stranger as I crossed the shared balcony to see if Mark had left the door to the kitchen open. It was also locked. When I reentered the neighbor's apartment, the girls had sensed my growing anxiety and one of them began to cry.

"Daddy is just sleeping hard. He's going to wake up any minute," I told them as I used the neighbor's phone to call 911. When I told the operator my concern and clarified why I didn't have a key, I heard the call dispatched as a "domestic." Twenty minutes later, a single police officer showed up. His reassurances were useless, as it was now almost an hour since we had arrived, and Mark had not materialized. The building's cleaning lady came to start her day, but she did not have keys to the apartments themselves. The officer told her to take the children outside while he broke down the door. I told my crying children to go to the car with the "nice lady" as I handed her my keys. She looked flustered but must have understood the desperation in my voice. She took my girls and my car keys, and I ran back up the stairs. I called my father-in-law and told him to come as quickly as he could. A sinking, nauseous feeling had set in. My hands trembled. The officer began unsuccessfully kicking in the door when the landlord, who the neighbor had called, finally arrived with a key.

I knew if it was suicide, I'd find Mark in the bathroom. Instead, I raced to the bedroom. There I found my husband, face down on the floor. I couldn't move him. I couldn't turn him over. He felt like a brick. I remember screaming and the police officer moving me out of the way. He couldn't get Mark to move either. He told me that Mark was gone.

"No!" I insisted, as I grabbed Mark's heavy hands in mine. "Look, his hands are still warm. Please, he's alive. I know it!" We managed to roll him over together. I gasped because Mark's nose was bloodied and bent. Mark was completely unconscious and I could feel myself going into shock at that point. From far away, I heard the officer yelling at me to start chest compressions while he called for an ambulance.

"Hurry!" he barked, "he's not breathing." The officer, who had been so quick to dismiss my fears just minutes before, started giving my husband mouth-to-mouth resuscitation. Then, as if it was as easy as walking out of the room, I walked out of my body and watched Jeanette continue giving Mark chest compressions. For forty-five minutes, this surrealism continued. Press 1, press 2, wait for breath. Press 1, press 2, wait for breath.

I watched myself whisper to him, "Please, Mark, please breathe. I love you, baby. Please, you have to breathe." I watched as the officer yelled at the medics, angry about what could possibly have taken them so long. I watched the officer physically pull me off Mark when the medics swooped in to do their work. Then came the emptiness of the flatline. I screamed and it was then that I snapped back into my body. I remember running then; pushing through the dark, dank hallway into the light outside, and filling my lungs with the cold. Gasping for breath and trying not to throw up. Shaking, I called my best friend, Stephanie, who lived in Boston, and my other closest friend, Kristin, who was impatiently waiting for me at work, wondering why I wasn't there to start our presentation. I couldn't find the words at first, just a wail. Then I got out to each of them that Mark was dead. Steph said she would be on the next flight out and Kristin rushed to her car. I had no idea where my children were but my father-in-law had arrived and apparently taken me back upstairs.

I remember laying down with Mark, holding his now cold hand and sobbing into his chest, screaming at everyone to get out and leave us be. It felt like hours later when I came to, and the officer gently but firmly told me it was time for me to go. That I had to be with my children. That my father-in-law had taken them back to his house and that I had to go to them because they were scared. He said I had to be the one to tell them what had happened. "It has to come from you. They need you."

Our children were five and nine on the day their father died. All they knew was that an ambulance had come, I was upset, and Mark was still sleeping.

"My husband and I were together for twenty-one years! Twenty-one years and I wasn't here for him. How could he die alone?" I asked the officer, over and over again, as he gathered my belongings and passed me off to my sister-in-law, who stood in shock. I hadn't even known she was there. I told him I couldn't leave Mark's body alone in this horrible place. This place that was not our home. This place that reeked of cigarettes in the hallway, shitty 1970s carpeting, of his death and my despair.

"I promise you I won't leave him alone, ma'am. I will stay with him and see him off."

That is how our love story ended.

Lessons Learned:
How to Cope in the Immediate Aftermath
of Losing Your Spouse

If you are a widowed parent reading this book and the worst has already happened, know you did everything you could to cope with the turbulence of being tossed into the sea when your life shipwrecked and your partner died. On the off chance you are reading this and preparing for such a loss of your loved one, the following are suggestions drawn from my own experience and that of other widowed parents that might help you to help yourself in the first hours and days after being widowed.

1. **If you are in a hospital when you receive news of your loved one's death, ask the hospital social worker or grief counselor for resources to help you through the first few days.** Many funeral homes can also connect you to your local bereavement center.

2. **Seek crisis support if you become overwhelmed, especially if the death is sudden.** Most larger cities and counties have a local crisis hotline you can call and ask for support. Many of the centers host mobile outreach units that can send a trained crisis counselor to your home, your children's school, etc. to support your family at this time. This is especially recommended if you are coping with a death from homicide or suicide. Another option available to all in the US, Canada, UK, and Ireland is crisis text support through the Crisis Text Line. Visit https://www.crisistextline.org/ or text HOME to 741741 (in the US) to connect 24/7 with a trained crisis counselor.

3. **Try to get to your kids first.** It's best for them to hear the news from you, even if you need help from a doctor or family members to find the words. See the chapter that follows on how I told my children the unimaginable.

4. **Surround yourself with people you love and who will look out for you and your children.** In most cases, people will want to come to your aid when they hear of your loss. If you feel up to it,

control who is there and surround yourself with those whom you trust the most. Put someone in charge of keeping others you don't want in your grief bubble out. Determine what decisions you feel capable of making and delegate those you cannot handle. If you can barely function, ask another adult to be in charge of caring for you and your children until you feel more yourself again.

5. **Do whatever you need to do to get through the first day.** If you need it and have another adult to depend on, ask your doctor for a sedative. Know that it's okay to hide yourself away in your room for hours. Check on your kids when you can and take them to bed with you if you need to that night. Take it hour by hour, day by day, week by week, after that.

THREE

A Family Gone Overboard

One in nine Americans will experience the death of a parent before age twenty[1] and yet most parenting books never fathom such a thing could happen in the normal course of family or child development. For me, finding Mark's body was not the most traumatic part of the god-awful day he died. It was what came next: telling our children. There are things I remember vividly in the hour or two after finding Mark's body. The way the frigid Buffalo air hit my face as my sister-in-law and I walked out of his apartment to her car. How I insisted she stop for coffee before we went to tell the children. I wanted them to have just a little longer before I shattered their world. I didn't drink any of the coffee, but I remember the way the heat stung my hands. Arriving at Mark's childhood home, I was acutely aware that the steps I was going to walk up to enter the house were the same ones Mark and I sat on in our teen years, sneaking kisses. As we entered the house, I recalled how the screen door always opened on the wrong side. Inside, I found the girls watching TV and I gathered them into my arms, whispering through my tears, "I'm sorry, I'm so sorry. He's gone." And then I have no memories of what happened next, until we were back in our own home.

---

1 Jade Richardson Brock and Craig Pierce, *Parenting Through Grief: The Attenuation Approach* (Createspace Independent Publishing, 2014), 1.

When our nervous system and brain become overwhelmed by fear, grief, or trauma, it is possible for some of us to dissociate—what trauma psychologist Bessel van der Kolk describes as not knowing or not noticing something that is happening to you.[2] Dissociation was not new to me. It was a tool I relied on during the most difficult times in a childhood punctuated with its own trauma. I hadn't needed it in twenty years, but I slipped right back into it that morning to get me through finding Mark's body as well as whatever words I said to my children about what happened in that apartment. Dissociation for me comes in one of two ways: either I black out memories or I hold onto a fragment of what is happening consciously while I unconsciously separate myself. It's almost like I can watch myself floating away from my physical body doing whatever it is doing at the time.

When we arrived home an hour, maybe two, after I had apparently told the kids about Mark's death (as they appeared as shocked as I must have looked to others), people had already gathered in our driveway. The school social worker, psychologist, and principal, bless their hearts, had walked over after someone (perhaps me) had called to tell them why the girls never made it to school that morning. My friend, Kristin, whom I had called before leaving Mark's apartment was there as well and she folded me into her arms. Over the next forty-eight hours, a police investigation was conducted into the cause of Mark's death, which was standard, as he had died alone. I prayed and prayed it wasn't suicide.

While I cannot recount the specifics of what I said to the children when I first told them of Mark's death, I do remember the conversation I had with them two days after he died. My home was still abuzz with people looking after us when someone picked up my cell phone and said the county medical examiner was holding the line for me. The medical examiner and I knew each other from a community task force we served on together. She gave me her condolences and said she was shocked to see Mark's name come across her

---

2 Elissa Melaragno, Trauma in the Body, 2018. "Trauma in the Body: An Interview with Dr. Bessel van der Kolk," *Daily Good News That Inspires,* last modified April 21, 2018. https://www.dailygood.org/story/1901/trauma-in-the-body-an-interview-with-dr-bessel-van-der-kolk/

desk. She told me she believed Mark had died of a rare condition called Sudden Unexplained Death in Epilepsy (SUDEP). I remembered reading about SUDEP in my research on epilepsy, but I was confused because Mark's doctors made it seem implausible. I asked if the seizure had killed him. She said it was not the seizure itself, and explained to me what she understood of SUDEP, alluding to a general lack of information on the condition. Most scientists believed it was something similar to SIDS but occurred with both children and adults who had epilepsy. She told me that there was a National Registry for SUDEP that I could enroll Mark in. Scientists and doctors at New York University who ran the registry would study Mark's case. They'd conduct a forensic investigation into his medical history, go through his autopsy for additional findings, and examine his brain tissue, if I chose to donate it. She said it might give us answers to what happened to him and help them make progress towards solving the mystery of SUDEP. Mark was an outlier. Most of the people who died of SUDEP were younger. I agreed to enroll him in the study. She said to expect it to be six to nine months before the results of the autopsy and investigation were available.

As I sat there thinking about how I could explain something that even doctors and scientists didn't have any full answers to, I knew my children needed to know something about what was going on. I asked the friends who had been caring for the girls while I was on the call to leave the three of us alone. I snuggled them close to me and found the words. I tried to be as concrete as possible. I told them that after the ambulance took Mark's body from the apartment, I gave the doctors permission to do some tests to find out why he had died. I explained to the girls that the tests showed that their daddy died from his epilepsy. They already knew that 'epilepsy' meant a sickness in his brain that caused him to be sad, that caused his hands and sometimes his body to shake, and that made him sleep a lot. At nine years old, Grace was keen enough and angry enough to demand more of the truth.

"But I don't understand. You both told us when he got sick that he couldn't die from epilepsy! You said it was a sickness in his brain but he couldn't die from it. Why did you lie?"

I pulled her closer and stroked her hair as she pulled away from me.

"I'm sorry Grace, we didn't know. The doctors thought it was the kind of epilepsy that death couldn't happen with, but I guess they were wrong. Your daddy and I told you what we knew to be true at the time. I know it's unfair and you have every right to be angry. I'm going to try to get us more answers. The doctor who did the test today said there are more doctors, epilepsy specialty doctors, who want to learn more about what happened to Daddy, too. So, I think we should help them learn more. They will call me soon and I will try to get answers to any questions we have. All I know now is that Daddy's brain and heart stopped working and he died. That means he can't wake up, he can't come back to us. And we won't see him again because he is dead now. Do you both understand what *dead* means?"

"Like Big Mama?" Veda asked mournfully, apparently recalling the death of her pet crab, whose exoskeleton we found outside her shell when she died.

"Like Big Mama," I repeated. Grace, who remembered attending her grandmother's funeral just two years before, said she knew death meant you can't come back. Veda then asked if my brain would stop working, too.

"No, I don't have epilepsy and neither do you. Our brains are working just fine. You do not have to worry about us, ok. We are safe. We are safe. We are safe." Then I asked if they had questions. The girls shook their heads and Veda asked if she could have a cookie. I knew that was enough information for the moment. I couldn't help but wonder if I had shared too much. While I never mentioned donating his brain tissue, did the girls at their age need to know about the study I was enrolling Mark in? Yet I also wanted them to know I was going to keep searching for answers—that I couldn't accept that his death was simply unexplainable.

Another few days went by and I finally decided to venture back into the world. I went in search of a book, any book, that would tell me how to help my children make sense of such a senseless thing. I could find nothing on parenting through such a loss as this. But I did recall somewhere I had notes in a box in my basement from another trauma therapist I had taken a class with. I couldn't remember her name, but I remembered she ran a child trauma institute. I went searching for her name and number, pulling out notebook after notebook from a box of my old coursework until I found what I needed. Elizabeth Davis, herself, answered the phone number I dialed. With a shake to my voice, I explained to her who I was and what my family was going through. I think the first exhale I took after Mark died was there on the phone with Elizabeth. Through my tears, I told Elizabeth that all I had wanted as a parent was for my children to escape childhood without great pain, given the traumas that had haunted me in my early life. As I detailed for her how the kids had been at Mark's apartment with me that morning and how, despite my best efforts to shield them from it, they had overheard much of what was going on, she said the thing I had to accept was that trauma is traumatic, meaning that it is wholly out of our control. Elizabeth stated, "You can't make trauma not traumatic. It is what it is. You've got to help your children face reality. If you are okay, your children will be okay."

Elizabeth went on to tell me that it was okay to show emotions and cry in front of the kids. She said, "No matter how much you tried to plan for protecting your children, trauma has arrived just the same." All I could do now was care for the children. She said I should take my cues from them about how to respond over the next few days to all we would face as we said our good-byes to Mark. She told me if I stayed stuck in my disbelief about his death, the children likely would, as well. Elizabeth shared, "If you shut down and refuse to talk about your real emotions, the children likely will, too. If you model openness, show your pain, show yourself seeking help and support, your children will be more likely to do the same." Elizabeth ended our call by telling me I was doing everything I could in the immediate aftermath to care for the children and that while she usually recommended waiting to start therapy for a period after an immediate loss, she agreed with my concern that my children needed an assessment for psychological first aid, given the events that had unfolded with them in the apartment the day Mark died. Before we hung up, I made an appointment for the three of us to see her the following month.

Lessons Learned:
How to Talk to Children About the Loss of Their Parent

There is no easy way to do this; just some suggestions from myself, grief experts, and other widowed parents towards lessening the blow.

1. **If you can, deliver the news of the death to your children yourself.** It's going to be gut-wrenching, but you can find the right words—your words, the words of a loving parent. If able, enlist other adults to help you through the experience of delivering such news but be sure to share with them ahead of time what you do and do not want said to your children about the death. They can sit with you when you deliver the news or be near to step in if needed.

2. **If you are anticipating the death of your loved one, involve your children in saying goodbye at an age-appropriate level.** For example, children over nine can usually decide whether they want to be present at the death of a parent if the loss is anticipated. Honor the child's wishes and do not force a child either way.

3. **Use simple, concrete language to describe what death means in a physical sense.** Explain the ways in which the body stops functioning. Share just enough so the children can digest the news. Invite them to ask questions but only directly answer those. Let them know they can ask you any other questions they have as they come up.

4. **If you do not have the specific information that children are asking for, be honest and tell them so.** Let them know how you or another adult will try to seek that information out and share it with them.

5. **If you are spiritual or religious and you think your children will find it comforting, you can add information about your spiritual beliefs and discuss with your children what they think of the afterlife.** Whatever your beliefs, assure your children the parent is at peace and not suffering.

6. **Remember, different children will react differently to the news.** Children's ability to grasp death will vary sharply by age and developmental needs. Teens may want to isolate themselves afterward while young children may immediately become clingy. Your kids might also get up and go back to playing afterwards, which is just a way for them to try to normalize and regulate overwhelming emotions. One sibling may take the news one way, and another respond entirely differently.

7. **Remind your children that in no way is the death their fault.** Children of all ages tend to blame themselves for things going wrong in families, as they are naturally egocentric. They need to hear you say early and often that this tragedy was in no way, big or small, their doing.

8. **Be the one to tell your children any new news about the death.** As more information becomes available to you about your partner's death, share it with your children first, so they don't hear it second-hand.

9. **Keep lines of communication open over time, even years out from your partner's death.** As children grow, they will reprocess the loss and may have new questions.

FOUR

Saying Goodbye

Like many co-parents and couples, Mark and I had never really discussed what to do if one of us died prematurely. Well— we had discussed it, but never arrived at any conclusions. Although we were both raised in the Catholic Church, Mark had come in and out of religious affiliations in his adult life and we did not have a church home at the time of his death. I knew that I wanted a wake for him, as so many of our friends and family were shocked by his death and would want to pay their respects. The only thing Mark had ever told me explicitly about his wishes, on more than one occasion, was that if he died, we should hold a party. He'd say it half-joking, half serious. "Jen, when I'm dead, don't do anything for me but light a fire and get shit faced! A real Irish wake. Call it the After-Mark party." I knew he'd want the Irish "water of life" flowing and now with him gone, I knew this is exactly what would bring me comfort: sitting around our backyard fire pit, surrounded with our closest friends, playing his guitar, toasting his life, and singing his favorite songs.

When I was awaiting determination of the cause of Mark's death (as mentioned in the last chapter), I was simultaneously having to make decisions about what to do with his body. Sometime in those first few hours after we had returned home, I decided we'd use the same funeral home for him that helped us when we lost the baby and when my mother died. After talking to the girls' school psychologist and social worker, I also made the decision that Grace and Veda would be given as much control and say in whatever mourning rites we put together as possible. Later that day, these professionals sat with the girls as I explained to them what would happen next.

"Tomorrow, I have to go to the funeral home and make decisions about how we want to say goodbye to Daddy. A funeral home is a place where the people we love can go to say goodbye to the person who died. We'll tell Daddy how much we love him and everyone who loved him will also come. They'll tell us how much they loved him and how much they love us. We will all cry for him because we loved him so." Grace asked if it would be the same funeral home that we had used for my mother.

"Yes, the same one. You remember how they have that room you can go to if you want to run around and play? You can be there and be as close or as away from me as you want to be. You can also come with me tomorrow to help choose how we'll say goodbye, or you can go back to school. Or you can stay here with our friends and not go back to school for a few days." As the next day was Halloween, Grace was worried about her friends missing her at the Halloween parade. Veda said she wanted to be with Grace. I wasn't sure what decisions I would make at the funeral home, but I knew I didn't want my children to feel left out of their father's funeral. I also understood it was not appropriate to place all the decision-making on a five-year-old and nine-year-old. I figured I'd formulate my plans and ask for their input. I was willing to change any plans they seemed upset by.

I slept for maybe two hours that night, my house full of the warmth of my girlfriends, three of whom came in from out of town and decided they'd stay for the first week. I had no words for the amount of gratitude in my heart that they would see us through that first week.

The resolve I felt about my ability to attend to the business of his death quickly slipped away as I sat with my father, one of my two brothers, Mark's father and his two sisters at the funeral home. Our first decision of that day was whether to cremate or bury Mark, and if burying him, where to put him. Then we'd have to decide on a wake and funeral. Almost immediately, the tension that had existed in my relationship with his family due to our marital separation came into the room. We couldn't reach a consensus. I couldn't bear the thought of making such a permanent decision when I felt so overwhelmed—a decision that meant my girls wouldn't have a chance to see their father's body again, if they needed that. On the other hand, the funeral director had informed us that the injuries Mark had sustained would likely still be somewhat visible, including on his face, if we had an open casket. I feared that I would make the wrong decision and that it would haunt our daughters for the rest of their lives. I ran out of the room, crying.

My brother, John, came out after me, reminding me that whatever we were going through in our marriage, we had not divorced and as such, the decisions were really only mine to make. He helped me to feel empowered when I felt like a puddle on the floor. I went back in the room and told everyone, including the funeral director, that I needed an hour alone with my children to discuss it all. I said I would have to come back that afternoon and would decide then. I left the funeral home, called the school, and talked to the school social worker, who agreed to pull the girls out of class and meet with us so I could ask them what they would like to happen to Mark's body.

When I arrived at the school, I told the social worker my dilemma and she helped me find the words to explain cremation in an age-appropriate way. I reiterated to the girls that when a person dies, their spirit leaves and only a body remains—a body that can't feel or think or talk or move anymore because it is dead now. I told the girls we had two options now that the body was dead, and both of them meant that the body would turn to dust.

"We could turn his body into ashes, which are a type of dust, or we could put his body in the ground, where it would turn back to dust over a long time. If we chose to turn it into dust now, we would put that dust, called his ashes, in a vase"—and I showed them pictures of the urns from the funeral home pamphlet I had brought along. "If we do this, you can touch the vase and people can say goodbye to his ashes before we bury the vase with his ashes in the ground at the cemetery. Or we could take his ashes in the vase home with us. We could also decide to put his body in a casket." I again showed them pictures and told them we would see his body before we closed the casket and put him in the ground.

Grace chimed in, "I didn't like Grammy in that box, because she had funny makeup." I was grateful the girls didn't ask how a body turns to ashes and I didn't offer to explain. We looked at the pictures of the urns again. I wanted them to understand that they wouldn't see Mark's body again if we cremated him. I asked Grace if she understood this. Grace became upset by this idea. She asked to see him. As we talked through the fact that his face had been injured from the seizures and that she might feel worse upon seeing him; we sadly agreed that it would be best to remember him as she had last seen him, just one week ago. The girls and I decided together to cremate him. I then gave them the choice of three urns, asking which they thought was best for Mark. They chose a black marble urn. Grace said it looked like "the right vase for a gothic rock star like Daddy."

Veda echoed, "Yeah, Daddy's a rock star in heaven now."

I also talked with the girls about his burial. Although we were no longer practicing Catholics, I thought Mark should be buried near his mother at our local Catholic cemetery. The girls were familiar with the cemetery and regularly had come with me in the last two years when I went to mourn my own mother there. The cemetery was also only a ten-minute ride from our house. It seemed logical to me that his ashes (or at least some of them) should be placed there. I asked the girls how they felt about burying Mark's ashes at the cemetery, some-where near their grandmothers, or whether we should bring them home or, perhaps, let them go somewhere important to Mark. Just a few months earlier, Mark had taken Grace on a special hike to an "eternal flame" within a waterfall at a nearby park. It was one of Mark's favorite places to hike.

Grace asked, "What if we bury half his ashes in that vase, near our grand-mas, and then take some to the eternal flame?" Just like that, she had provided the answers I needed. Hearing her assuredness helped me make up my mind on another issue I had been wavering on: whether I should reserve a plot for myself with Mark. His father had already pointed out that, as we were separated, he felt Mark should be buried with his mother, instead of with me. But sitting at the school with the children confirmed for me that they should have their parents together, if not in life now, then in our deaths.

Before I left their school, the girls and I had decided we only wanted to deal with the wake once, so there would be a one-day formal wake on Sunday after-noon, followed by a memorial service at the funeral home and then the Irish wake/Rockstar Daddy party for a limited number of guests immediately afterwards at our home. Grace said she wanted to come to the funeral home and asked if she could do something special for Mark during the service. I told her I'd help her decide what to do. Veda clung to me and agreed with everything her sister said. I knew she was coming to the wake either way. Other than going to school that day, she hadn't let me out of her sight since I had told them what happened to Mark.

I kissed the girls and told them I had to go back to the funeral home. I told them we would go trick-or-treating when they came home from school and in the morning, they could help me pick out all their favorite pictures of their dad to share at the wake. I don't know if it was just to soothe my conscience or if it really will have come to mean a lot to the girls that I included them in these decisions, but I was grateful to have centered them in my decision-making. I left the school feeling slightly less overwhelmed than when I arrived. I called Mark's family and told them of my decisions. If anyone disagreed, they didn't voice it.

The next 48 hours were a whirlwind of preparations. Mark had died on Thursday and we would have the wake on Sunday. I had yet another task before me. If we were not to have a religious funeral, the memorial would have to be filled with something. Mark and I were both writers (and tragic romantics). I knew I wanted to be the one to write his service, even if I couldn't lead it. I look back on those first few days now and wonder how I got through them. I remember that night, but its effect is softer now; it makes me long to hold the woman I was then, to stroke her hair and whisper to her of her strength, her courage, her intellect. All the qualities she would need to call upon in the months and years that followed.

I wrote multiple tributes to Mark in those early morning hours. One to be read at the funeral home, one a toast for my beloved during the Irish wake, and the other to be read at his burial later that week. I struggled most with which words to say at the burial and then it occurred to me: he had already given me the words. I ran upstairs and went through box after box of old papers until I found it: the poem he had written and read on Halloween Eve, four years to the date before his death, when we buried our baby's ashes. I modified it slightly, but his own words were the blessing I needed to usher him on his journey. I also decided that night that I would not wear the same black Calvin Klein dress I wore to my mother's funeral. Instead, I would rock the electric blue dress that he had just bought for me to wear to his sister's wedding—picked out on that last date, just a few weeks prior.

That Sunday, over 400 people came to Mark's wake. I remember thinking how he spent so much of his life feeling unloved and, yet, here was proof of our community's love for us. People I never expected to see from various former lives we had led were there. Friends from high school we hadn't spoken with in almost twenty years embraced me and my children. Many of Mark's clients from his days working with people with developmental disabilities, along with many of his chiropractic patients, came. Most people there didn't know that we had separated or even that he had been ill with epilepsy. Part of me felt like a fraud. Did I even have the right to call myself his widow? Hadn't I been the one to leave? On the other hand, a separation isn't a divorce and we had been actively working on healing our relationship. I decided it was not necessary for me to explain myself or our relationship to anyone, but I also no longer felt I had to carry these secrets anymore. I realized then that something was already shifting in me because of the grief. I felt a rawness to life; a vulnerability that hadn't existed the week before my loss. Whatever Mark and I were going through, it melted away in those first days. All that mattered to me in those moments was that his life was honored; his children must know how much their father was loved, how much he loved them, and what good he did in the world.

To help myself and the girls get through what was sure to be an epically long day, I had asked my friends to take different supportive roles. One would be stationed with Grace and one with Veda. Another would be stationed near me so I could give her "the look" when I needed to be rescued and taken away to a private room to cry or catch my breath or hide from someone I didn't care to see. Grace and Veda kept their eyes on me but stayed far away from where I was positioned next to Mark's ashes. We arranged to have a space set up in another room in the funeral home for the children to get away from the crowd if they wanted. They had snacks, toys, comforting books, and blankets. Two other friends left the wake early and went back to my home to prepare the food and drink for the Irish wake that would follow. My friend, Kristin, presided as a lay minister for the service.

The four longest hours of my life came to a close with the sharing of Mark's favorite poems, readings, and prayers. Grace read an Irish blessing for her daddy. I held Veda throughout the service, and she started stroking my tear-stained cheeks as we all cried our way through singing Mark's favorite Avett Brothers song, "Swept Away," the one he had intended to play for his father-daughter dance with Grace at her one-day wedding. They had sung it frequently together and he would accompany her on his guitar. As the song reached its crescendo, I started to crumble and couldn't get the words out. Mark's closest friends, Amy and Erin, held me and sang the words even louder as if his proxy. They held me until the crowd started to thin. Then we all transitioned back to our home to begin the After-Mark party. The girls' regular babysitter offered her services for the evening to tend to the girls and any other children who came with their parents. I needed to know they were being cared for, but I also knew I needed to finally let myself begin to grieve the loss of my husband. The girls stayed near me for the first hour or two of the night as the singing, drinking, and storytelling to memorialize Mark continued. The sitter eventually got them settled with a movie and off to sleep so that I could be loved by our community.

Community is the balm that covers our wound and allows us to start healing. I was never so grateful in my life for the community of friends who lifted the girls and me up that day and week. My best friend was on an airplane within two hours of his death. One of my closest friends from college got on a train within hours of my call, even though it was the first time we had connected in three years. Another drove eight hours to get to us. Many of the people that came to the Irish wake I have not seen since, but it meant everything to me that they dropped everything else in their lives that day to join in with the whole of Mark's community and shower us with love.

A few days later, at the cemetery, I gave the girls the job of distributing roses to our friends and family. Veda took her job as an important one, despite the cold November day. I think it kept them standing to have a focus and task for the ceremony at the graveside. The girls returned to my side once everyone had received their rose. Everyone received a white rose to lay on Mark's grave, but the three of us had red roses to remember our love. As I watched my brave little girls lay those red roses on their father's freshly dug grave, I was hit hard with the knowledge that there was nothing I could do about their pain but continue to be there with them in it.

Lessons Learned:
Creating Safe Spaces for Grieving Children
During Memorials and Other Rituals

One of the best things I did for my kids at both Mark's formal wake and his Irish wake was to make sure they had spaces just for them. Here are some ideas to help you carve out a space-within-the-remembrance space that can support your children's physical, emotional, and spiritual well-being. Such safe spaces can also be useful for children when visiting a dying parent in hospice or the hospital.

1. **Prepare your children for what such a physical space looks like** (whether this is in a funeral home, your own home, a cultural center, a hospice, etc.) If you are able, show them the physical space beforehand. Explain to your children that you will be there for a good period of time and that you want them to be comfortable there. Ask them what they need to be comfortable (e.g., can they bring a comforting blanket or stuffed animal? Their favorite snack or a device with headphones and a movie on it? A favorite memento or picture of their parent who is being remembered?).

2. **Ask your children to identify adults who they love who can support them if you are unable to be fully present with them.** Is there a favorite aunt, uncle, or family friend who can help care for them during this time and be someone to provide respite if they need to get away from the adulting happening around them?

3. **Keep in mind that older children may want their safe space to be inclusive of their peers.** Maybe your teen would like to be stationed outside the funeral home, hanging in the parking lot with their friends. Or maybe they'd like to be in charge of creating picture memorials or digital shows for a service. Let your older school age children and teens take charge of what they need to feel involved and supported during meaning-making.

4. **Consider that some kids may need a "grief-free" zone.** For some children, it will be too emotional for them to process the death of

their parent in such a prolonged space and time, such as a three or four-hour wake or if sitting shiva. Allow your children to tell you when they've had enough and help them find a "grief-free" place to go for any remaining time you are remembering your spouse.

PART II

Treading Water

FIVE

Our First Days
in the After

If there is ever a time we need to be mothered, it is in deep grief. As I moved through those first days and weeks after Mark's death, it settled on me how very much I missed my mother. I wished, more than anything, she was there to help me and the girls through that awful time. Instead I settled for the love of my friends, my brothers, and my father. A day or two after the memorial services for Mark, each of my friends from out of town and my brother boarded a bus, train, or plane, and headed home. The girls and I were alone for the first time since he died. I suppose it was lucky that I had accrued a whole six weeks of vacation and sick time. I decided to take it all and not return to work until just before Christmas.

The kids went back to school, and I filled my first days alone with the business of Mark's death. There were people to call, the apartment to empty, his car to sell, and $150,000 of student loan debt that I fervently prayed would be canceled. I pushed through the days even though they were consumed with worry. While I made good money at my job, I had paid Mark a substantial amount of alimony in the year prior, which had emptied my savings account. One of the things we had fought regularly about that year was his inability to adult. He had never set up life insurance, even though I frequently asked him to, and when he tried to get it after his diagnosis, it was too late. No one would insure someone with epilepsy. His retirement savings cashed out at $314. *What now? What next?* These questions grew loudest at night as I struggled to sleep as much as my girls did.

We were all afraid to close our eyes and turn ourselves over to the magical forces that guided us safely from sleep to waking. Grace asked the first night after Mark's death and Veda repeated it regularly: "What if we die in our sleep, too?"

"We are safe," I'd remind them, as much as to myself, as they lay in my arms each night in my bed, which they had both immediately moved into. We'd watch episode after episode of *Cupcake Wars* and silly animal videos on YouTube, often until 2 a.m., until we finally caved to our bodies' need for sleep. I was exhausted, physically, and emotionally. I didn't recognize myself in the mirror, but it wasn't the worst thing. I had lost fifteen pounds in less than fourteen days since Mark's death. My body forbade any nourishment to my system. My spirit was crushed, and I felt just about ready to give up on this life myself. *What now? What next?*

I felt unmoored. I told myself this would be a period in my life where I just had to tread water and keep my head above the waves. Dry land seemed miles and miles away. Even though I kept reassuring the children we were safe, I didn't feel safe at all. The dissociation I had experienced on the day he died frightened me. When it happened in my childhood, I was never conscious of it. But now I was, and I was very afraid I was going to mentally crack. My mind kept surveying the ocean, all the blue in front of us, looking for something, anything to hang onto. I wanted something or someone to carry me to shore; to answer what was next.

You can imagine my relief, then, when I found her. Google had informed me on one of those sleepless nights that there was a Meetup group for widows and widowers a few towns over. As I browsed the group's information, I noticed that one of the administrators, Erika, looked younger than the rest. I decided to message her, pouring out my story. She messaged me back promptly, despite the late hour, with a "Here's my number. Why don't you call?" As can happen with other people who have been through similar circumstances, I felt an immediate kinship with Erika and I clung to all the practical advice she shared about navigating all the death to do's. She told me there was a Meetup that coming weekend and she thought it would do me good to come. "Make yourself get out of the house, even when you do not want to." Then she laughed, nervously, saying I needed to know she lived above a funeral home because it was a "great big, cheap apartment that no one wanted."

As I dressed for the meeting, I laughed at myself, first dressing in black and then changing into a red top. I put on lipstick for the first time since Mark's funeral. As I sat in Erika's driveway, debating what entrance was hers versus the funeral home, a woman popped her head out the upstairs window and her now familiar voice beckoned me up the side stairs. I walked into Erika's apartment and found a room full of broken souls. Most looked to be in their late sixties or seventies, but Erika was definitely in her forties, I surmised, along with one other woman. There was one guy who looked to be in his mid-to-late thirties like me and two or three people probably in their fifties. As they each went around introducing themselves, I learned some of the people, like Dolores, had been coming to the group for a while. She shared that this was her eleventh year without her husband. I thought, *God help me if I'm still coming here in eleven years.*

I was relieved to not be the only newbie. Brian, the guy who I later learned was also thirty-six, had lost his wife two months before Mark had died. This was his first meeting, too. Brian just shook his head when it was time to share his story. He couldn't even get the words out. He looked at me, indicating I should share instead. I got as far as, "My husband, Mark, died two weeks ago..." and the hot tears started to flow. I couldn't stop sobbing. Someone got me tea. Someone else gave me tissues. Another held my hand. These people, who I had judged as soon as I walked in, had survived the shipwreck. Some of them were just barely hanging on, but others, they threw us newbies a life preserver. As we mingled after the large-group share, one person after another came up to me and hugged me, telling me how strong I was and how I would survive this. Another told me I needed to start eating and made me a plate of food to take home since all I could still do was nibble. Many of the women offered to assist me with childcare. I left Erika's house two hours later with a pocket full of phone numbers and emails, as well as a promise to return. I let out a big, deep exhale when I got back in my car and quickly gobbled up the plate of food upon my return home.

The relief didn't last long. A few nights later, I woke up to throbbing pain in my left hand. I turned on the light and stared at my hand. My ring finger was blue. *Shit*, I thought, *I should never have put the rings back on.* The guilt I felt about Mark dying while we were separated had led me to put my wedding ring, my engagement ring, and a promise ring Mark had given me when we were twenty, all back onto one arthritic finger. I pulled at the rings, but they didn't budge. I went downstairs and got out a jar of olive oil, pouring it liberally on my hand. I couldn't even get the rings to spin. I tried butter and then soaked my hand in hot water and cold water. My finger looked like a big, blue sausage. I turned to the trusty internet to tell me what to do next. *Elevate your hand above your heart. Seek medical assistance.* It was 3 a.m. The pain worsened and I called my father frantically. He arrived and stayed with the girls while I drove myself to the ER. Neither the nurse or two doctors could remove the rings and I heard them in the hallway discussing my plight. They called the fire department. A nurse found me sobbing into my pillow and said, "There, there, honey, it's just jewelry. I'm sure your husband will buy you another ring." When I told her what had happened to my husband, she held me and let me cry onto her shoulder. Big, fat tears fell as she patted my back and said she was so sorry for her careless words. I reassured her that she couldn't have known. She stayed with me as the firefighters came with their special tools and cut the rings off my finger. The doctor who discharged me said I was lucky they got them off when they did as I could have lost my whole finger due to how badly the circulation had been cut off. "No more rings," he said, as he handed me a plastic baggie with the remains of my wedding bands.

When I got home in the early dawn, my father said he would stay a bit while I slept. When I woke up that afternoon, I felt numb again. While I knew the rings were "just jewelry," it seemed to me that everything and everyone who had meant something to me kept being taken away. The rings were one of the few possessions from Mark I had cherished since his death and now they were destroyed too. My father broke through my fog. "Jeanette, are you listening to me? You're one lucky girl. I found you a plow service that can start tomorrow." Lucky, sure. I looked out into the backyard and saw the patio furniture still sitting out as the snowflakes started to fall. Fresh tears started upon the realization that Mark wasn't coming to put it away for the season as he had agreed.

The shock of it all still caught my breath. No, there was nothing lucky about me or my life now. As my father continued to drone on about the plow and how he had put a shovel outside the back door because there was a snowstorm brewing, I stared blankly at him and pretended it meant something to me. I kissed him goodbye, as he said he wanted to get home ahead of the storm. Erika and I chatted for a bit later that day as I recounted the early morning's plight and then the girls and I settled into another season of *Cupcake Wars*.

I was awakened by gleeful laughs and screaming in the morning. The girls showed so little joy since their father's death, I was confused but excited to see what all the commotion was about. "Mom! Mom! Mom, wake up! Wake up! The whole door is covered in snow! The whole world is covered in snow!"

Huh?

I made my way downstairs and looked in disbelief. When I saw that the snow did indeed rise about six or seven feet high, completely encasing the front door and the side door, I stopped smiling. I have always had terrible claustrophobia and being unable to exit the doors made me panic. I ran to the dining room and saw the windows were also all covered in snow. Same situation with the exit out of the house from the back porch. We were completely trapped. It had taken all of my willpower every day for the last two weeks to function and not lose my mind. And now this. I hadn't seen a snowstorm like this since I was a young child. I deemed this fresh hellscape Snowmageddon. The dictionary actually has an entry for Snowmageddon, referring to it as a storm so severe it disrupted everyone's daily life. Some in Buffalo still prefer to call it "Snowvember." Some fool, the County Executive to be exact, called it Winter Storm Knife because it cut the metro area in half. Guess which side we lived on?

My answer as to what to do now was the same as all folks traditionally do in Buffalo when snowed in: I drank. The first day I tried to keep it light. I let the kids watch TV all day and night, praying we didn't lose power. I kept drinking because everyone who came to the After-Mark party brought the widow wine [with their platitudes]. I drank just enough to get through the second day and still be a functional parent as I grumbled about how the last thing I needed was a snowstorm on top of all the other grand shit that had happened in the last few weeks to us. That night tormented me, though, with thoughts of the house caving in on us, so I kept drinking just enough to numb the added worry. By the third day of the "blizzaster," roofs all around us were, indeed, collapsing, including the roof on the girls' school. People were dying from the storm. The local news reported that at least two people had succumbed to heart attacks while shoveling snow. Later that afternoon, I watched out the window as an old man was carried down the street on a stretcher by other kind men, as the ambulance couldn't make it down the street. *Maybe that wouldn't be so bad*, I thought. Let them take me away. But who would care for the girls if I gave up?

A few hours later, I pressed a fresh glass of wine to my lips, as I watched my garage roof crumble in on itself. It seemed like a sign from the universe. I wondered if the porch roof, which connected to the bedroom where the kids and I were sleeping (or not) would go next. How would we survive this? If there actually was an imminent threat to our lives, I should probably do something about it. I felt like a helpless child again, unable to solve my own problems. I called my dad, who said to sleep in the center of the house, so down I moved us to the dining room. I blew up an air mattress and we tried to sleep (but mostly didn't) under the dining room table, thinking it would provide extra protection from a crumbling house. Finally, around 2:00 a.m., the girls fell asleep, just in time for the panic to creep back in. It was in that moment, lying there in the dark, listening to the wind howl and watching the street lights flicker, that the weight of the last two weeks hit me. Disbelief ran through me again. How could my husband of twelve years, my friend and love of twenty-one years, be gone—never to walk back into our home to hold me again?

The permanence of Mark's death washed over me the way the waves in Lake Erie catch you in an undertow; with water in place of breath. I refused to accept what was evident. I was left on this earth to figure out how to raise these grieving children alone, without their father's love. Without their father. So, I poured myself more wine. And in my brokenness, I reckoned with God. Or rather my lack of belief in one. Because when you're drunk, you'll talk to a god, any god, even a god you don't believe in. If you've seen the movie, *Forrest Gump*, it was definitely a Come-to-Jesus-Lieutenant-Dan-on-the-Shrimp-Boat kind of moment. And I had nothing good to say to Jesus, His Father, or the Holy Ghost

I was taught to believe in during my childhood. I sobbed. I silently screamed in my widow wail way (the kind where you are sobbing so hard no sound even comes out because you can't catch your breath), and I begged this God I wasn't sure of that if She or He or It would take my husband, to let the ceiling crush us tonight, and reunite us with Mark. Even though I had a community caring for me, I had never felt so alone. And just as God did for Forrest Gump, God answered me. I had left the TV on in the living room, hoping it would lull me to sleep. It was then I heard the words, "You are the only gladiator in this place."

I had a choice to make at that moment. I could choose to remain this way, waiting to join Mark, riddled with guilt about our separation and his dying alone, terrified to continue my life without him, and helpless to change my path. Or I could summon the courage to start over. Instead, I passed out.

With the light of dawn, something inside me shifted. I felt, for the first time in two weeks, that maybe, just maybe, I could swim out of this storm— this storm I had unwillingly found myself in, where the word "widow" was whispered. Where my children no longer smiled. Where people left casseroles in a cooler outside my door—at least when I could still find the cooler or the door. Peering out the window, I could see that the snow was still piled above our heads. We were still trapped. It was day four of the storm and seventeen days since Mark died. It was the day I chose to begin again.

I took some Tylenol for the hangover. I got a bucket from the laundry room and a ladle from the kitchen. The snow had melted just enough that I could push the side door open just far enough to scoop a bit of snow into the bucket. I made it a game with the girls. How many buckets could each of us scoop? By the afternoon, I was able to open the door a full two feet and find the shovel. By evening, I had dug a path to the street. We couldn't go further than that, but we could get out of the house in an emergency. I could breathe again. For the first time in my life, I didn't physically or emotionally depend on anyone else to save me. I had rescued us.

That night, I didn't drink. As I tucked the girls into the air mattress, still sleeping under the dining room table, we made a bucket list of all the things we dreamed of doing to honor the lives Mark would want us to live in his absence. Veda would get her ears pierced. Grace would try out for a musical. I'd take them to Broadway and Paris. I'd swim in a waterfall and buy a piano. To honor his life, we would live ours beautifully and courageously. Finally, I slept.

On day five, I awoke and decided it was time to figure out what was next. We scraped by with the last of the casseroles for dinner. Day six brought friends, one wielding a backhoe who cleared half my driveway, and two more who spent four hours digging out my car. The girls and I feasted on a box of Triscuits, Laughing Cow cheese, and the last pack of my very favorite junk food, Zingers, found on the otherwise emptied shelves of the convenience across the street. I decided it was a sign from Mark. He knew they were my favorite and often ran across the street for me in the wee hours when I had a hankering for them. Erika and Brian, from the Meetup group, both checked in on me. I remember telling Erika I felt paralyzed by the fact that I would have to make all of the decisions alone now. If Grace had an asthma attack, Mark wouldn't be there to listen to her lungs and tell me whether she needed to get to the ER. Who should I call to repair the garage and what the hell would I do when the next thing in this ramshackle house fell apart? I told her how his landlord at the apartment had called and gave me until Thanksgiving to clear out all of Mark's stuff. How, I asked her, was I supposed to bring his things home but not him? "One day, one decision at a time," she said.

I repeated my new mantra to myself that night. *You are a gladiator. No one is coming to save you. You have to save yourself.* The next morning, I decided that as soon as the snow melted for good, I was putting the house up for sale. Five months later, I would do just that.

Snowmageddon came to represent the period of deep pain and personal struggle I faced in the days and weeks after Mark's death. *How much can one person take?* This is a question I asked myself over and over again in those first thirty days after his death and throughout the first year. Although I decided to start over on the fourth day of the snowstorm, to summon all of my strength and surface from the icy water so I could get my bearings, my grief for Mark, combined with the weight of all the earlier losses sucked me down dark cold holes. Sometimes I would vacillate, hour-to-hour, minute-to-minute, in the belief that God had abandoned me. I was being punished for my sins, from past lives or the present one. It is so easy to sink into a pit of self-pity and despair when confronted with the very inconvenient truth that we all will die one day, while simply trying to live our lives. Just as you can choose to begin again on any given day, life as you know it can also end on any given day. It shouldn't take death to wake us up to the business of really living. While we survived that literal storm, it was just a few dark nights in a much larger, churning ocean. Nothing had prepared me for being a widowed parent at thirty-six, even though I had spent the three years preceding Mark's death in deep grief. I thought I knew the storm. I had no idea I was about to enter the eye.

But what of a child's first month living through tragedy? Like me, my children were living in a state of shock and denial for the first few weeks. So much had happened and so much change was looming. I knew that the literature on children and loss broadly suggested that in a crisis, all children, regardless of developmental age or stage, needed structure, first and foremost. When everything in their lives feels like it is spiraling out of control, some structure, any structure, can be a stabilizing force. The girls had gone to school only a handful of days in the first thirty days after Mark's death due to the time they took off to attend his services and then the snowstorm that followed soon after. As the roof of their elementary school had collapsed in the storm, they wouldn't return to school until the first week of December. First, we would have to get through Thanksgiving. Our second holiday without Mark. Grace echoed my sadness. "Grammy used to love making Thanksgiving dinner. Then Daddy took over. Now what?"

Gladiator Jeanette told herself she could surely get it together enough to cook a Jennie-O turkey breast from the grocery store down the street. A few hours later, Exhausted Jeanette remembered there was a reason she had never cooked a turkey before, as she cleaned glass shards and dark meat out of her oven. "I'm so stupid!" I said to myself in disbelief. My lack of experience in cooking led me to forget to spray the pan with oil. In an attempt to redress the situation, I poured cold water in the hot glass plan thinking that I should unstick the turkey breast from the pan. When I heard the boom and saw the mess that I had made of our sad little Thanksgiving dinner, I puddled again on the kitchen floor and once again called my father for help. We ended up going out to dinner for the first time in our lives on that Thanksgiving. The girls enjoyed the buffet, while my father, brother, and I pretended that half of our family wasn't actually missing from the table. I remember wondering if my kids were really okay. On days like this, they seemed normal enough, in spite of the persistent feeling that normal was robbed from us a month ago and normal would never come again. We did, however, have a routine. Routine was the word echoed by all the clinicians I spoke with about children's bereavement. When Grace and Veda went back to school in December, routine is what I provided. As the girls and I had been living as just we three before Mark's death, we slipped back into that familiar schedule. They went to school, they came home, we played, we made something to eat, we watched TV, they took a bath and went to bed. Once a week, the school social worker checked in with Grace. We only varied our evening routine to take Veda to see her counselor once a week. The counselor was a child psychologist that Mark and I had just taken Veda to for the first time the week before his passing to complete an assessment. Veda had been expressing a lot of anger towards me during our separation and had taken to some newly aggressive behaviors, like biting and slapping. When Mark died, I called the psychologist and said I had a new problem to add to my kids' pile of problems. She agreed to keep seeing Veda for play therapy to help her cope with the loss on top of the original issues we were concerned about.

Over the weeks that followed, I got comfortable asking for and accepting help because I felt overwhelmed by all the to-do's ahead of me. Some friends helped me clean out the apartment. I asked for and accepted help from other friends and family to babysit the girls so I could deal with selling Mark's car, setting up stand-by guardianship, Social Security benefits, and shopping for Christmas presents. My father helped us haul a Christmas tree into the house at the kids' request. It was smaller than usual, and I ran out of the room crying as they placed ornaments from Mark's childhood onto the tree. We got through that day and all the days leading up to the holiday. I didn't have to ask, only accept the help when one of Mark's best friends, Erin, casually said to me, "What are you and the girls doing on Christmas Eve? Want me to come and help you do gifts and stuff when I get out of work?" I gladly took her up on the offer and she and I cried as we wrapped gifts and listened to the record that he had made me the year before, his last Christmas gift to me. Twelve songs he recorded with his indigo blue acoustic guitar and his beautiful, sad voice singing love songs, hoping to convince me to stay.

I dreaded seeing family on Christmas day for dinner, as was our tradition, so the girls and I started a new tradition. We went to see a mid-day movie and then rushed to Mark's sister's house, just in time to sit down to her dinner. We were out-the-door as soon as dessert was served, as I explained we had to pack for our trip in the morning. I had never traveled alone with the kids before but as the holidays loomed, I knew I desperately needed to get out of Dodge. I took up the offer from Steph and her wife, Haley, to join them in Boston for the remainder of the school break. As the girls dozed on their first Amtrak train ride, I cried remembering the many times Mark and I had made that same trip. Our life at twenty-two had seemed like it would reset in Boston and here I was, at thirty-six, returning without him. At midnight on New Year's Eve, sheltered in the warmth of my friends' home, I cried with them as we rang in the New Year. I mourned for Mark. I mourned the end of 2014: the last year in which he was alive. I still didn't know what came next, but I knew I had made it through two months without him. The work I was doing on myself the year before his death and in those first two months after, especially my revelation during the snowstorm that I would need to start over, and meeting a room full of folks who understood what it meant to lose a spouse, set the groundwork for what came next: the search for dry land.

Lessons Learned:
A Checklist for the Newly Widowed

I found myself overwhelmed by all that was before me in dealing with the "business" of Mark's death. Although I didn't come across this checklist for the newly widowed until I was a few years out from my loss, I immediately saw its usefulness. I hope it helps you. It has been reprinted with permission from the Soaring Spirits Loss Foundation, in partnership with the Liz Logelin Foundation.[3] Please note that this list is not an all-inclusive roadmap. It is not intended to be used as legal advice nor should it be considered a substitute for a meeting with a duly licensed estate attorney. It will, however, provide you with some tips that may make things easier in the weeks and months ahead.

1. **Allow people to help you.** They want to, and you will need them. Ask them, if necessary.

2. **Write things down.** Your memory might be unreliable for some time.

3. **Delegate.** Many of the next items on this list can be done for you by someone else.

4. **If you have a life insurance policy, contact your agent or company immediately.** This will ensure that you have funding for the funeral expenses. The funeral home often will coordinate with the life insurance company. Check with your employer regarding whether you have a bereavement leave benefit available.

5. **Check with your spouse's employer to verify whether there is a company-sponsored life insurance policy in place for your spouse, obtain the current information regarding any applicable 401K accounts, and check the status of your health insurance if your family was covered by your spouse's employer.** There may be a grace period when you will still have coverage, but you will

---

3 Reprinted with permission of the Liz Logelin Foundation and Soaring Spirits Loss Foundation. For more resources to support young widows and widowers, visit http://thelizlogelinfoundation.org

want to find out the exact date that any changes in coverage will apply. If you have joint investment accounts or investment accounts held in your spouse's name, these will need to be addressed.

6. **Get at least 5-10 certified copies of the death certificate.** There are many agencies that will require an original document when they are notified of your recent loss. You will also need to carry a death certificate (and your child's birth certificate) with you if you are traveling internationally with a minor child. Be aware that you are charged a fee for each copy of the certificate you order.

7. **If you live in the US, notify your local Social Security Office and have your spouse's social security number on hand.** Warning: Many of us were horrified when we discovered that there was a one-time death benefit to surviving spouses of $255. Obviously, this amount does not come close to reflecting the value of a life. If you live outside of the US, please check the Liz Logelin Foundation (LLF) resource page or contact the LLF for assistance with finding the social services information that applies to the country in which you live.

8. **Have someone help you.** You'll need to sort through office paper-work to look for personal accounts, outstanding appointments, upcoming trips that may need to be canceled, or anything that must be dealt with before a cancellation charge applies.

9. **If applicable, locate your spouse's cell phone.** You may want to preserve their voicemail message in another form, as it may be deleted accidentally if the phone malfunctions or the service contract ends.

10. **Make a complete list of your spouse's credit cards, debit cards, phone cards (checking their wallet is a good place to start), business expense accounts, and any other open accounts they may have.** Each of these institutions needs to be notified of your spouse's death, and many will require a copy of the death certificate to validate your request to close the account. Also ask each company whether there is any applicable insurance that pays off

the account in the event of a cardholder's death. Check auto loans, credit cards, and mortgages for this type of insurance.

11. **Keep an open file within easy reach for your health insurance in case there are expenses associated with your loved one that are yet to be paid.**

12. **Check your utility bills to be sure all of your utilities are in both of your names.** Most companies require your name to be on the account before you are able to act as administrator of the service. One thing to be aware of: companies often have to shut the service down and then restart it in order to change the name on the account.

13. **Make banking changes after you have a death certificate in hand.**

14. **Cancel any recurring membership fees or annual magazine subscriptions that apply only to your spouse.** Adjust any that applied to both of you.

15. **Make changes to emergency contacts as necessary.** The children's school contact form is especially hard to change, but also vitally important.

SIX

Overthinking Grief:
Mine and Theirs

U pon our return from Boston, I decided a new year meant it was time to
take baby steps in answering the question: *What's Next?* Firstly, it was time
to return a semblance of normal to bedtime. The girls weren't ready to leave my
bed yet, but I told them no more television until all hours of the night. I pulled
out some of Mark's favorite childhood books from his boxes and read them
Cinderella, Alice in Wonderland, and *The Swiss Family Robinson.* This description
of the shipwreck in *The Swiss Family Robinson* stayed with me and was the
inspiration for the title of this book:

> *The nearer we approached the land, the more gloomy and unpromising
> we thought its aspect appeared. The coast was occupied by barren rocks,
> which seemed to offer nothing but hunger and distress. The sea was calm;
> the waves, gently agitated, washed the shore and the sky was serene; in
> every direction we perceived casks, bales, chests and other vestiges of
> shipwrecks, floating around us.*[4]

---

4 Johann David Wyss, *The Swiss Family Robinson: The Journal of a Father Shipwrecked with his Wife and Children on an Uninhabited Island* (London, Blackie and
Son Limited; Translated from the German of M. Wiss, 1905) 17.

Sixty days of treading water was exhausting. If I had learned anything about myself in my life, it was that staying stagnant would not help. I needed to re-root myself, starting with a new house. Everyone (and I mean *everyone*) that I shared my thoughts with about moving repeated the same words to me: *Do you think it's wise to make such a big decision so soon, Jeanette? I hear you really shouldn't make life-altering decisions like that until you're at least two years on.* Was there a hidden record about how to grieve that all of these people not immersed in the murky waters of deep grief were listening to? It is highly likely that you, like me, not only heard such a phrase but also, well intentioned people in your life probably recounted the five stages of grief to you, too. *Denial. Bargaining. Anger. Depression. Acceptance.* They seem to be a universally accepted paradigm, at least in America. One of them must include the instruction not to make big decisions in the first two years. I sighed. Murky waters = big emotions; I got that part. But were there really *stages* to how I would move through my grief? I hadn't experienced them during my other losses. Maybe I hadn't had time to process each one before the next loss had happened. Perhaps with this one, I'd feel differently.

With nothing but long wintry nights stretching out ahead of me, I spent a lot of time house hunting on Zillow and a lot of time thinking about my own grief process. Even though I had a graduate degree in Human Development and Psychology, the only grief model I was really aware of when I was widowed were these five stages of grief, first theorized by Dr. Elisabeth Kübler-Ross in her 1969 book, *On Death and Dying.* Kübler-Ross had based her model on her observations and interviews with terminally ill people who were preparing for their own deaths. She wrote of the five stages that they were an attempt to share "what we have learned from our dying patients in terms of coping mechanisms at the time of a terminal illness."[5] As one of the co-founders of the Hospice model and the death with dignity movement, her expertise was essential in pushing back on the western ethos, fueled by Sigmund Freud and the two world wars, that death is something to be hidden away and not talked about. That said, her famed book does not discuss in any depth the experience of the

---

5 Elisabeth Kübler-Ross, *On Death and Dying* (Scribner; Reissue edition for 50th anniversary, 2014), 35.

bereaved; at best, it examines the reactions of family members to news of a loved one's terminal illness. As I went through early bereavement, the stages popped up again and again, usually in the words of people who tried to comfort me and in my own attempts to make sense of what was happening to me.

"You're in shock," more than a few of the women who attended Mark's memorial said to me, as they leaned in to give me a too-long hug. After the third or fourth time hearing it, I remember wanting to scream: *No shit, Sherlock. My husband just died! That's him, right there, a pile of ash in a fucking urn!* Instead, I'd reply with, "Thank you for coming. You meant so much to Mark." As I stood there next to his ashes, I was completely aware and accepting of the fact that Mark was dead. Wasn't acceptance supposed to be the last stage? While I was not in denial about his death, it was true that my body and mind had experienced shock. So much so that just 72 hours before the services, at his apartment that morning and then later when telling the girls about his death, I had dissociated.

Could shock and acceptance co-exist?

Where did anger factor in?

"You might feel angry, honey," said the nurse at my doctor's office. I had left the Marital Status check boxes blank. She prodded and I explained my husband had died. As she took my blood pressure, her face soured and she continued, "When my cousin died, I was so mad that the good Lord took her so soon. She was 72 years young. I don't think I've ever really gotten over it. I know what you are going through."

Do you, though? Did you love your cousin the way I loved my husband? Did you leave your cousin the way I left my husband? Have you cried until your body cannot make more tears? My body would bristle, and my chest would tighten whenever people started to tell me of their losses when they struggled to know what to say to me about my own. The five letters that made up the word 'anger' were not sufficient to describe the rage that was lying just under the surface of my skin in the first half of 2015. I would experience many breaking points of my anger during the next few years, but none that my children would remember as much as the first one.

Sometime after the holidays, I had to return a pair of expensive jeans that had been gifted to Veda. They were too big and while the receipt wasn't provided, they still had the tags on them. I simply wanted to exchange the jeans for the correct size and was relieved to find the right size on the rack. As we waited in line behind a number of other customers, I watched the young cashier argue with every person in front of me, also apparently making returns. I grew more and more agitated. When I reached her and tried to explain my situation, she stopped me quickly and said she couldn't help if I didn't have the receipt. "Look," I said, "they were a gift for Christmas. I don't have the receipt, but you can see the tags are still on them. They are in the original bag and they clearly haven't been worn. I just want to trade down a size."

"Listen, lady, I told you we can only take a return with the receipt. You'll have to come back another time," she countered.

"You listen," I said, my heart rate and voice rising. "I'm already late for dinner. I am a single mother. I don't have time to come back here on a different day and the person who gave them to us as a gift can't find the receipt. Could you please just help me out and let me exchange them? I'm not asking for cash back; I just want to trade this pair for that pair." She glared at me and waved her hand dismissively.

"Next!" she said, looking through me. Something snapped. Suddenly, all the anger I had been suppressing since Mark died fell out of my mouth. A voice I didn't recognize as my own bellowed, "Just give me the fucking pants! God damn it!" I screamed as I threw the pants across the counter, and they landed on the cashier.

The parents behind me took their children's hands and backed up. My children stood there with their mouths agape. The cashier's mouth was, too. I grabbed the girls' hands in mine and now that my anger was out, I couldn't put it back in. I continued my tirade, as I dragged the children behind me, stomping out the door.

"Fuck you!" I screamed behind me at the cashier, the racks of clothes, and the stunned families. "You are not helping me. I'm sick of this shit. Everywhere I go, I have to do everything myself. Fuck you and your stupid fucking store. I will never come back here. You hear me, bitch?" I hurriedly put the kids in the car and drove off, tears streaming down my face. I kept checking the rearview mirror, as if the cashier was going to call the police and start a crazed widowed-woman hunt. I had never in my life acted out with such anger, or such language, in public. The girls didn't say a word the whole way home as my anger turned to embarrassment and then eventually to laughter. I wondered if my children thought I cracked as I pulled into the driveway, laughing with tears rolling down my cheeks. Today, whenever my kids sense my temper coming on now, one of them will surely say, "Let's hope this isn't going to turn into another pants incident." I never did set foot in that store again.

In the first year, I could have these moments like the one described above. Little things would trigger rage, seemingly coming out of nowhere. I would occasionally allow myself to admit I was angry with Mark for dying. Later in 2015, when the autopsy results finally came in, it showed there was no evidence of medication in Mark's body at the time of his death, but his toxicology report was positive for marijuana and alcohol. When I stopped crying, I left the house and drove straight to the cemetery. Stomping through the snow, I let all the heat rise in me as I yelled at his grave, "How could you! How could you! Why would you do that and leave me here? Didn't you know this could happen? Why did you lie to me about the medication and the seizures? Why didn't you take care of yourself?"

Mostly, I felt sad and lost in the weeks and months that followed. Inevitably, my anger at him would turn to guilt: Why hadn't I forced him to come home that night? Why hadn't I checked his medication? Why had I left him to deal with this illness on his own? Why had I been such a bad wife? I'd explode and then stuff it back down so I could function.

In Kübler-Ross' model, bargaining, with depression on its heels, would come after the anger. It seemed for me, though, that bargaining went hand-in-hand with depression and anger, generally also accompanied by a medical crisis. I remember how, on the way to the emergency room, steering with one hand while I held my other hand with the blue finger high above my heart, I whispered, "Please God, don't strike me down with a heart attack or stroke right now. Let Google be wrong. Please don't let me lose my finger. Please God, I will stop being angry at Mark if you just let me live through this and not orphan my children."

Anger turned to bargaining turned to acceptance seemed to move through me quickly. One night, I had to rush Grace (during another blizzard, of course) to the emergency room for an asthma attack. I bargained with God all night. The next morning, as Grace rested on the couch and her sister played quietly next to her, I lost my shit again as I tried to start the gas snow blower for the first time ever on my own. After several attempts of it not starting, I directed another "Fuck YOU!!!!" at it. Then I screamed at the snow. "Fuck YOU!!!!! I fucking hate Buffalo! And fuck you too, Mark, for not being here to do this. Fuck all of YOU!!!!" I screamed into nothingness. I gave the start one more strong pull and the blower roared to life. I cried as I ran the machine all the way down to the end of the driveway where it promptly puttered out of gas.

"I hate all of this," I muttered to the snow, as I plopped myself down in it and cried and cried. When I got up, the girls were standing in the doorway, looking frightened at the sight of their mother, forlorn in the snow pile. As I had done so many times before, I brushed away my tears and went in to take care of them.

Was that acceptance or just giving up? Could I cycle through the five stages so quickly while just attempting to snow blow the driveway? I'm pretty sure I accepted the fact that my husband was dead the day I chose the marble urn that would hold his cremains for eternity. I accepted that he wasn't playing a game with me or off on a business trip. He was dead. I had seen it with my own eyes and had tried to save him with my own hands. I couldn't change the fact that Mark was dead. All I could do was accept it. But what of my life and the girls' lives? Was I supposed to accept this is how we would stay? A distraught mother, cursing at everyone and everything that didn't go her way? Children who were going along for the ride, worried that it was only a matter of time before something happened to her, too? Clearly Kübler-Ross hadn't been a widow. If she had, exhaustion would have been a sixth stage.

When I could think about my grief from a somewhat detached perspective (was this numbness?), I could see that I was experiencing each of the five stages as emotions, or states of being, but there were a lot of other big emotions as well. Certainly what I was feeling felt nothing like a stage with a finite beginning and ending. If anything, I felt like I was experiencing them all, all of the time. One night, someone in one of my grief support Facebook groups shared this image:

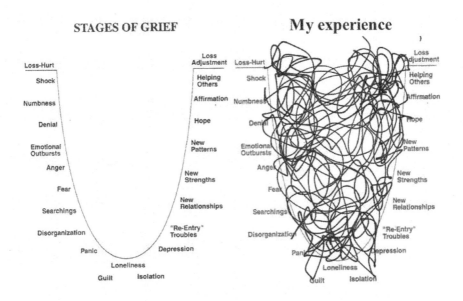

The squiggle seemed to be an Internet meme, with no known origin[6]. That didn't make it any less real to me. If anything, the squiggle felt more like my experience of grief than the linear Kübler-Ross model. My grief squiggle was probably done in an angry red crayon.

What else is there outside of Kübler-Ross' model to help us create a frame or structure for understanding how we will process our grief? One of them was, literally, right in front of my face. Early in that new year after Mark's death, I was at work and observing one of our foster care caseworker training programs.

---

6 Anonymous as seen in Bluffview Counseling Services. "We Have A Right to Grieve Losses Big and Small."(March 31, 2017). Retrieved October 18, 2023.URL: https://www.bluffviewcounseling.com/we-have-a-right-to-grieve-losses-big-and-small

That morning, as I was chatting with the trainers and helping to set up the room, I looked up and stared at the statements on the wall that one of them had just posted on a large sheet of flipchart paper.

1. Accept the loss

2. Acknowledge the pain of the loss

3. Adjust to a new environment

4. Reinvest in the reality of a new life

Of course! I recognized these statements in our training as the Tasks of Separation, which, over the course of ten years as a curriculum developer, I had written into countless training manuals. But at that moment, I was seeing them with new eyes. For our purposes in child welfare work, we had reframed them as tasks of separation but the reference reminded me that they came from William Worden's theory on the tasks of mourning.

Worden first posited these tasks in 1982 in his seminal book, *Grief Counseling and Grief Therapy*. In an interview in 2013, Worden said that these four tasks of mourning are the things that need to be accomplished by the bereaved after the loss of a loved one. Next, the interviewer asks Worden how his tasks are different from Kübler-Ross' stages. He notes that Kübler-Ross was studying the dying and that her staged model was created for how dying people experience grief in relation to their death. It was never intended by her to be a model for the bereaved. He knows this, as he had conducted research in collaboration with her in his earlier days.

> *"By using the task model, which comes from developmental psychology, the tasks have a certain fluidity, they can be worked and reworked. Some are very easy to accomplish and others can cause some people some problems. But it's a good model. Because if someone is stuck in their grief, it gives you (speaking to grief counselors) an overlay to figure out how they're stuck and why they're stuck and how to help them move on."*[7]

---

7 Worden, J. William. "William Worden: The Four Tasks of Mourning." June 6, 2013. Springer Publishing, 2 hours, 2 minutes.

Worden's task model is also called the TEAR Model of Grief. T=To accept the reality of the loss. E= Experience the pain of the loss. A=Adjust to the new environment without the lost person. R= Reinvest in the new reality. Did the TEAR model apply to me? I felt that I had accepted the loss as well as one could, just a few months into it. I was daily acknowledging the pain of that loss while adjusting to life without him. There were two major ways in which this was happening for me. First, the parenting of our children changed overnight. I had gone from having my weekends to fill as I pleased the year before to suddenly being a solo parent. Although he struggled to give 100% as a parent due to his physical and mental health issues, Mark was always there for the girls when they needed him. Even when it was difficult to talk to each other, he and I made decisions together about the girls. Our world, whether we were together or apart, moved around the axis of our children's needs. Now he was gone and I was with them, 24/7. I had never been more scared of getting something wrong. I knew from the first morning that how I handled Mark's death and our bereavement, for good or bad, would have life-long implications for our daughters. Secondly, I had to adjust to the Mark-sized hole in my heart. I had not only lost him as my co-parent but I had lost the person I loved for twenty-one years— who had given me the validation and care that I had needed but not received; who had taught me there could be beauty and joy in sexual pleasure; who had loved me when I thought I was not worthy of such things and who, I, in turn, loved when he thought he was not worthy of such things. And I would also have to grapple with this same man being the one who I resented for his failures as a partner; who could hurt me as much as he could hurt himself; who had spent our life together predicting he would die young and now here I was, alone. What would my reinvestment in the reality of a new life look like?

There is one other older model of grief that I learned about in researching this book that I found applicable to my own life at the time. It is Lois Tonkin's model of growing around grief. Tonkin, a grief counselor from New Zealand, had observed that, for many of her clients, their grief did not end; they simply adapted to it. In her brief publication on her model in 1996, Tonkin noted that most theories of grief had a culminating point; an end after a series of steps or stages were completed by the bereaved.[8] But this wasn't holding true with what Tonkin witnessed as a grief counselor. She reported that some of her clients never achieved "resolution" of their grief. In her theory's publication, Tonkin recalls attending a workshop with Elisabeth Kübler-Ross. She tells the story of one bereaved mother in Kübler-Ross' workshop. The mother, who had lost her child, said that the size of her grief had stayed the same. It did not lessen over time, as some expected it to. What happened instead was that she realized she grew around her grief.

Discussion of Tonkin's model is often accompanied by an image of a stone in a series of mason jars, in which the size of the jar (representing your ability to cope with the grief and transform your life) changes, even though the stone in the jar, representing your grief, does not. This made sense to me. In the beginning, my grief felt all-consuming. I couldn't get through an hour without crying. Somehow, just eight weeks or so later, I was crying only once or twice a day. I wondered if my tears would stop soon. Then what would happen? And even more important to me, what would happen to my children if we just outgrew our grief?

One of my most prominent worries after Mark died was how the children would cope with his death. Would such a profound loss at a young age forever change the trajectory of their lives? William Worden produced some of the earliest research on children's bereavement and grief process. Applying his TEAR model, Worden believed that children, like adults, must go through these tasks of mourning a loss: accept the reality of the loss, experience the pain or emotional aspects of the loss, adjust to an environment in which the deceased is missing and relocate the dead person within one's life, and find ways to memorialize them.[9] He also noted that children will have to re-attend to these tasks at different points in their development and reexamine their relationship to the deceased parent during significant developmental transitions. Worden and other researchers on children's bereavement suggest that there are no "typical" ways

---

8 Lois Tonkin, "Growing around grief—another way of looking at grief and recovery," *Bereavement Care*, Volume 15: 1, 1996.
9 J. William Worden, *Children and Grief: When A Parent Dies* (Guilford Press, 1st edition, 2001), 12-15.

children grieve as there are a number of factors that also influence this process for kids such as the child's age and cognitive stage, cultural background, religion, and cause of the death.

I knew enough about general child development to know that school-age children, like my own, generally comprehended death as permanent even though the idea of an afterlife could be elusive. I also knew that Veda, being on the younger side of school-aged, might still engage in some forms of magical thinking. Even Grace, at almost ten years old, might regress into such beliefs if it would comfort her.

When Mark first died, some of the most touching tributes we received came from the kindergarten and fourth-grade students at Veda and Grace's elementary school. They said things like "I didn't know your dad, but I know you and you are special, so he must be too" or "My heart hurts for you, my friend" with a drawing of one weeping child holding hands with another. While the children in their classrooms provided care and empathy to my children in the immediate aftermath of Mark's death, these children really didn't know what to say or how to relate over time to my children's experience. More often than not, the kids were coming home feeling more and more isolated.

During this time, I continually asked myself, "What do Grace and Veda need right now?" Tuning in, I'd watch Veda startle when fire trucks rushed down our street, on the way to another family's emergency. Each morning, Grace would visibly shake for a few seconds while we neared the side of their school closest to Mark's apartment complex, which you could see situated behind the school parking lot. I could tell they were pulling in on themselves, emotionally.

I was relieved when our appointment with Elizabeth Davis finally rolled around. The blizzard and its subsequent cleanup had pushed everyone's schedules back. While the kids enjoyed her office's play therapy room, I sat sobbing in the tiny room adjacent to it, telling her what I was observing in Grace and Veda's behaviors since Mark's death. We also talked at length about our marital separation and what the kids may or may not have witnessed on the day Mark died. After spending a little time with each child, Elizabeth agreed that Grace needed more help than the school social worker could provide to process what happened—not only to Mark, but to her, on the day he died, and as our family moved forward. She would start seeing her in the new year. Given her younger age and that Veda was already connected to a therapist, Elizabeth recommended that Veda stay with the therapist she had just started seeing.

Before leaving her office, Elizabeth reminded me of the old adage I knew about getting through a crisis. *What do you do if your plane is on fire and starts to go down? When the oxygen mask dangles in front of you, you secure your own first. Then you focus on others.* According to Elizabeth, for the newly bereaved to care for their children, they had to first start with self-care. As I bundled the children back up, she asked me who I was seeing for therapy. I assured her I was still seeing my therapist weekly.

"Good," she said. "Give yourself a heaping amount of grace." She advised me to whittle our lives down to meeting the bare minimum needs. Eat. Sleep. Cry. Go to school. Work. Therapy. Make the move. Eat. Sleep. Cry. Go to school. Work. Therapy. Ask for help. Accept help. So that would be the plan. A whittled down life until we all felt like more could be possible again.

It sounded easy enough; often, it was not. I found that what helped me most when I fell down, down, down into the cold, dark ocean of my grief was to simply surface, take a breath, and pause. When I had collected myself, I could reach in the dark and pull the children to the surface too. In the beginning, all we could do was sputter and cling to the remnants of the boat: the lives we once lived. I recognized immediately that the pieces could never go back to the way they were constructed before. I remain grateful that after the initial day of dissociative episodes, my faculties came back and my adult brain mostly functioned. Even when adrift, I could pull us forward by relying on what I knew from my training in crisis intervention and child development to help me navigate what to do next to keep us afloat. I knew that this knowledge was a blessing. I was luckier than many parents who did not have such resources. I also found that I started immediately tuning into my intuition in a deeper way than I ever had before, as you'll read in the next chapter. From the first day forward, I asked myself the same questions the experts did: what do I need right now? What do my children need? Then breathe. Then pause. If the answer that came wasn't going to help us survive, I let it sink back into the bottom of the abyss. All we could do at that time was survive day-to-day.

I'll revisit grief theory in the later chapter on how my children coped with grief over time including new research on the multidimensionality of grief, and even a model for transforming personal tragedy into community protection, like superheroes do. What all of these models of grief have in common is that, in order to adapt, both children and adults have to grow around our grief. We have to behave in different ways than we have before. We have to accept the change that has met us in an ambulance bay, or in the middle of the night, whether we least expected it or waited with bated breath and a watchful eye for our loved one's final breath. Grief is a process. It has big emotions that will wash over us, ready to cope with the tidal wave or not. We have to go, as the Buddhist nun Pema Chodron has written in one of my favorite self-help books, to the place that scares us. We must answer this question in our bereavement: "Do the days of our lives add up to further suffering or to an increased capacity for joy?"[10] At the heart of our mourning, we have to choose whether and how to begin again.

---

10 Pema Chodron, *The Places That Scare You: A Guide to Fearlessness in Difficult Times* (Boston: Shambhala, 2001), 9.

Lessons Learned: Getting in Touch with Grief

Sometimes we feel numb from our grief. Sometimes we feel overwhelmed by it. Sometimes we want to hold it at bay, as long as we can, to keep the dam from breaking. These tips were created by me, for me (and others, who asked me for help), when I was thinking hard on the process of grieving. I hope they will help you answer some of your own questions about your grief.

1. **Assess where you are with your emotions.** Try to get outside of your own head. What would your best friend say about how you are doing with your grief? What would your deceased partner say? What would another widowed person say? Take a hard look at your behaviors. Have you been numbing your grief with alcohol, drugs, or sex? Have you been avoiding it with busyness? It's okay if you have, so long as you aren't hurting yourself, your kids, or someone else. Be gentle with your assessment but be honest.

2. **Assess what's working well for you and your kids right now.** Write all of these things down. Who are the people helping you? Combined, these are your strengths and assets.

3. **Ask yourself what's not working so well for you and your kids right now.** Write them down. How are these things connected to your loss? Write that down, too. For example, if one of the things not working well is that you are working too much because your finances have been stretched without your partner's income AND your kids are having problems because you can't give them the attention they need right now, note this. You don't need to do anything about it now but recognize the loss. Take stock of the challenges really facing you. This may seem counterintuitive to detail ALL of your struggles and problems but it's important to really recognize how much your life has been impacted by the loss of your partner and co-parent. Each of us is struggling with the primary loss of our person but also losses that result from that person's absence.

4. **Pick one thing from your list of what's not working well. Maybe it's the most pressing need. Can you give yourself some space to sit with it?** To focus on it. To let it putter around in your head unabated. Maybe you can take it to therapy this week. Or talk about it with a friend or a trusted relative. Name the emotions you are feeling. Let them sit on your tongue. Let the tears come if they need to come. Try not to turn it off prematurely. Lean into the discomfort, even if it causes further anxiety. If it feels too overwhelming, reach out to one of your resources for support. Let yourself grieve this piece of your loss. Then do it again with another piece of your loss. And again.

5. **Assess where your body holds your grief.** It took a two-week fever for me to tune into the fact that I had exhausted my body. You don't have to do anything right now but notice where and how your body is holding your grief. When you feel up to it, consider trying yoga, stretching, reiki, or massage to tap into the pain your body is holding and help to let it go.

6. **If you are missing your person, write down all the things you wish you were doing together; the things you will miss out on in the future; the pieces of your past with them that haunt you.** Sometimes when we look deep at the pain, we are afraid we will be swallowed whole by it. It's easier to avoid. But we can hold our truth before us and let the feelings ripple over us like the tide. They will lap and recess. Lap and recess. Each time, the feeling will be felt and released.

7. **Try not to avoid the situations or triggers that make you feel vulnerable.** Dig out your wedding album. Put on the mix tape and listen to the old love songs. Pull up the good memories and talk to friends about the bad ones. Give yourself permission to look at the reality of the person you lost. What were their best parts? What parts were not the best?

8. **Some people find it helpful to revisit places that were special to them or their person; and/or to visit the grave or other**

memorial site. Sometimes we need to face the reality of the situation, even if for no other reason than to remind ourselves of what we have lost and to let that pain come again.

9. **Some people, especially if they have had earlier trauma or their loss involved added traumatic components such as a violence, accidental death, suicide, homicide, or any circumstances that are stigmatized, may need professional help processing their emotions.** Cognitive behavioral therapy and Eye Movement Desensitization and Reprocessing (EMDR) therapy need to be guided by a therapist, but both have shown evidence of powerful healing. I needed some intensive trauma therapy to process all I had lost.

10. **Find a ritual that helps you (and your kids) safely destroy something.** Renovate your house. Create art by smashing something into small pieces. Garden. Destroy so that when the time comes, you can create again. Anger needs an outlet, even if we do not always recognize the need for such. Sometimes it's not until we are knee deep in the mud of it, that we recognize what is stuck. Make sure you make room for your children to let their anger out as well. A punching bag is a good investment for holding a family's anger.

11. **Do not rush your grieving.** Do not expect too much else of yourself when you are deep in it. Meet yours and your children's basic needs: let them eat microwaved chicken nuggets and boxed mac and cheese for a year if that is all you can handle because doing this emotional work takes all your energy. Make the processing of your emotions a priority. It is often said that grief is the price we pay for love. Deep love = deep grief. Give yourself the gift of grieving well, even if you don't think you are.

PART III

Reaching Dry Land

SEVEN

Something Resembling Self-Care

I must have still looked shell-shocked when I walked back into the gym that January, two-and-a-half months after Mark's death.

"What happened?" was all my boxing instructor, Joe, could ask, bewildered, when I finally showed back up. I was at a loss for the words to explain it all. One of the things I appreciated about Joe was that we didn't talk about much but boxing during my lessons. Part of why I felt ready to return to our lessons was that I desperately needed a reprieve from talking about Mark and his death. I just wanted to hit something or someone and, after all, that was what I was paying for. Joe was also not the kind of guy who was going to give me a hug. When I shook my head and said it was all too much to talk about, Joe simply responded by wrapping my hands and giving me my gloves.

"Put these on, it's time we started sparring for a full session."

Usually, my lessons consisted of a warm-up, practicing jabs and kicks on the bag, and maybe five-ten minutes of sparring where I got comfortable learning how to take and give a punch. This time, we'd spar first. We danced around each other for a bit; I could see he was trying to figure out where I was emotionally and whether the two months off had impacted my skills. I answered him with a strong hook to his side.

"You let your guard down," I grinned.

"I did, and I won't make that mistake again," he said, as he answered my hook with a jab that I blocked.

For the next ten minutes, I moved. I breathed. I punched and I kicked until I fell in a heap crying. Joe was not my therapist.

"Get up. Get some water. Shake it off. We're starting again in two minutes."

This was exactly what I needed. Joe didn't pity me. Joe and the gym were there to hold space for me to work it out.

Self-care Saturdays, which I had originally implemented when I was flying single the year before, were back. Once I had used all of the free babysitting offers people made after Mark's death, I asked my father to take over caregiving for the kids regularly on Saturdays. I needed to spend every other Saturday hitting Joe. While my anger often felt like hot coals with nowhere to go but my mouth, when I was in the gym, the heat came tumbling out of my hands.

"You keep going like this, you'll be ready for a real fight in the ring soon," Joe said. I felt strong for that one hour a week when the rest of my life felt overwhelming. I gave myself permission to take a full day on Saturdays for me. One of the things I knew to be true from my earlier losses is that each of them took a psychological and physical toll on me. I had just pushed through them as if my life would recalibrate— as if my baby, my mother, and my friend could all die and I could just go on dealing with the ins and outs of everyday life without missing a beat. If there was a gift in the year Mark and I were separated, it was that I had found myself. Even though the separation was fraught with stress, I grew stronger during that time. When Mark died, though, I knew the pushing-through-it had to stop. I had worked hard to get this new sense of myself and if I didn't protect her now, I would lose her too. What would happen if I lost my identity and Mark at the same time?

Alice, my therapist at the time, and I talked about this. *You have to put on your oxygen mask first. Give yourself the gift of a break. You don't have to figure out what comes next. Just take a break from the present stress. That's enough now.*

On Saturdays when I wasn't boxing, I'd try to book a riding lesson. Sometimes after leaving the gym or the farm, I'd go to the library and pick up a book. Sometimes I'd go to the mall and wander aimlessly with a coffee and my credit card. I relished the car rides to and from wherever I was going on Saturdays as they were the only time I was really alone. The other six days a week it was the girls and I from dawn to dusk. When I was alone in the car, I'd put on the songs Mark and I loved (or when I was angry at him, I'd put on other songs to tell him how I felt) and I'd let myself really feel the feelings. Inevitably, the tears would start, and I wouldn't have to stop them to attend to anyone else's needs. Sometimes I'd drive myself to the cemetery, where I would sit on the ground next to Mark's grave and talk to him. I'd let myself feel sad or angry for a few hours a week. Sometimes, instead of visiting Mark in the cemetery, I'd find myself in Brian's bed.

Brian was the widower with the sad eyes at the Meetup group. After meeting that November and chatting a bit on Facebook during the snowstorm, he had disappeared for several weeks from both the in-real-life Meetup and the online group. Mark had only been gone a few months when I realized I was really, really missing sex. My guilt wouldn't bring him back so I figured I might as well try to feel something good again. I couldn't fathom how to start dating, though. My dating life to that point had consisted of two or three weeks-long "relationships" with teenage boys before I met Mark. Mark had been my life for twenty-one years. During our separation, I did a fair share of flirting and testing of the emotional waters with other men and women, but I had never slept with anyone else. One night, I lamented to my friend, Erin, that I felt horrible admitting it but I needed to get laid. I got it in my head that I wouldn't do so until after Mark's birthday in February—which functioned like a bookend of where he and I stopped and someone else and I could possibly begin.

So, when Brian returned to the Meetup group and his sad gaze held mine just a little too long, I boldly asked if he'd like to grab a cup of coffee after the meeting. He told me he had plans that day but suggested we meet the following Saturday instead. I spent the whole week hemming and hawing over what to wear. An hour before we were to meet, he texted something like an apology, telling me he had gotten called into work.

"You have to work on Saturday mornings? What do you do?" I asked.

"I'm in tech," he responded.

I decided he wasn't ready for the coffee but a few days later, he messaged me asking to try again the following Saturday. And once again, he texted me, this time as I was on my way to meet him, to explain that he had to attend to an emergency at the office. I decided that even the idea of being alone with another woman since his wife died must have been too much for him to consider. I dropped it and didn't reach out again. Two weeks later, though, he called me on the phone, which was his first. I picked up and we spent an hour talking about how we were doing. He told me a little more about his wife, Leah, and how they had been building their dream home when she died. She was only twenty-eight years old. He asked if we could get coffee the following Saturday.

"Look," I said, "I really appreciate getting to know you and the other folks from the Meetup. But it doesn't seem like you're really ready for that step and to clarify, it's not a date. I just enjoy talking with you and everyone else is so much older than us."

"Yah," was all he replied. And after a long pause, he said, "I really did have to work those two Saturdays. I have a jackass of a boss and when the network goes down, I get called in. I didn't mean to blow you off. How about we try one more time next Saturday? I won't be mad if you say no, given I've been a jerk."

"Okay then," I replied.

I, of course, overanalyzed what getting coffee this time meant, since Brian was the one to ask. That week, I decided that perhaps I should just be honest with him. He seemed like a straight shooter. He wore his grief heavy on his body, but underneath I could imagine how attractive his smile was. He lived nearby and didn't have kids to juggle. I had gone so far as to draft an email (in case the coffee meeting went well) explaining my needs and how he could be a good candidate for helping me meet them, if he was willing to meet a few requirements, such as getting an STD test.

I brought the draft email into therapy and handed it to Alice.

"Oh, Jeanette…" and she burst out laughing. I was hurt. "Jeanette, I'm sixty-two and I've been married for more years than I can count and even I know this is not the best way to go about bedding a man." I admitted I was struggling with it. I told her I wanted more than coffee with Brian. As we talked through my favorite word, Guilt (with a capital G), Alice asked why I was ashamed to admit I wanted to get sexually involved with someone.

"Mark has only been gone a few months. What will people think?"

Alice reminded me I didn't need to explain myself or my actions to anyone. No one had to know if I was pursuing a new relationship unless I wanted them to know. "Think of it as another form of self-care. It's literally just coffee. Leave it there. Given he seems a little unsure himself."

It was blizzarding (again) as I pulled into the parking lot at a local cafe on said Saturday for a third attempt to meet Brian for coffee. I looked around for the big red truck I remembered he drove. No truck. *This is miserable,* I thought to myself about the weather, my life as a whole, and to top it all off, this particular Saturday turned out to be Valentine's Day. And I was likely to be stood up by him again, as there was no sign of Brian inside the cafe either. I had just convinced myself to turn around and go when I got a text saying he was parking. *Big inhale.* It was just coffee. For me, at least. Brian went through four cups of cocoa (what kind of grown man has cocoa-binges, I wondered) as we sat and talked. He was quiet; almost painfully shy. Looking at his mug more than he looked at me, he told me about his life with Leah. I told him a little about the complicated relationship I had with Mark and how our girls were doing. I asked if they had wanted children. He told me they had been trying for their first when she died. Then he shared more with me than I think he meant to.

"I couldn't have handled it if she was pregnant when she died. I don't think I would have gone on if that had been the case." His eyes started to water, and I reached out my hand to his.

"It's okay. I'm so sorry." He withdrew his hand, tucked his vulnerability back in, and we talked about our mutual travels with our spouses to London instead. I told him I was struggling to go through Mark's things but should probably do so before we moved. He told me to call him anytime I needed an ear. The snowstorm was becoming so bad that the cafe decided to close early, so we took our cue to leave. Brian and I hugged and went our separate ways. I kept the email in the draft box.

A week later, I was broken down again on the front porch, having attempted to open the boxes that held Mark's bachelor life at the apartment. This shirt in my hands he had worn to Veda's dedication ceremony at our church. This record was from his favorite band; I recalled the time the car had been towed because he parked illegally to get closer to the concert venue to see the band. These were his favorite Doc Martens. I sat sobbing on the floor and Brian just happened to text at that time, letting me know he was having a rough night too. I called and we talked for two hours.

"How about I take you out sometime?" he said. "You deserve a night out."

"Okay," I replied. "That would be nice."

Later in the week, we made plans to meet at a local bar. Was this a date? I asked all of my girlfriends. They decided it was.

"I don't think so," I said. "He's not ready."

"He's a man," Erin said. "He's ready."

I repeated Alice's words over to myself throughout the week. *It's self-care, really.* In case it was a date, I decided I should get my hair and nails done. Nothing in my closet said *I'm interested but not slutty.* After buying some new jeans and a t-shirt, I found myself at a lingerie store.

You are getting way ahead of yourself, Jeanette. It's just a drink. I told myself he'd likely cancel, but the day we were to meet, Brian sent a text saying he was looking forward to meeting later that evening. This better be a date, I thought as I totaled my receipts.

"Mommy is going out with some friends tonight. She needs to relax," I told the girls as I got them bathed and into pajamas for the sitter. Once again over-thinking, I told myself I would not be the kind of single mom who had men in and out of her house and her children's lives (judgy, I know). I could go on a date or two, but I had no intention of bringing anyone home to my kids.

Brian was at the bar before I had even left the house because the sitter was late. When I rushed into the bar, I saw that he had saved me a seat despite the crowd. It was hard to talk over the noise, but we chatted a bit about him having moved into the dream house he was supposed to have lived in with Leah. I kicked back a glass of wine quickly to help calm my nerves because he seemed to be looking at me differently this time. He made more eye contact and I felt heat in the space between the bar stools. I excused myself and ran into the bathroom to splash cold water on my face. I was a lightweight drinker, and the one glass must have made me loopy. I suddenly felt both overwhelmed by the prospect of what could be about to happen and anxious about it in a good way. When I returned, I sipped a second glass of wine more slowly and could feel myself pulling away a bit from his stare. I kept sneaking peeks at him as my gaze moved around the bar. What would it be like to be touched by another man? How was it that I was thirty-six years old and had only ever had one lover? Would I hate myself or would the ghost of Mark hate me for wanting this man at this moment?

"Hey, what's wrong?" Brian asked.

"It's just...sometimes I feel guilty for moving forward with my life. I mean, with the house going up for sale, and all and even being here with you…" I trailed off and then the tears started to spill again. Brian hugged me and let me literally cry on his shoulder. I started to laugh then. Here we were at a bar, on something that might be a date. This was my first night out since Mark had died and I was crying in front of everyone and slobbering on Brian's shoulder. As I tend to do when overwhelmed, I stared down at my feet. Brian took my hand and when I looked up, he brushed the hair away from my face, touched the tears on my cheek and leaned in to kiss me. It was a really nice, sweet kiss.

"It's okay to miss him and it's okay to do what you have to do for you," he said gently.

I laughed nervously. "So, I guess this is a date, then?"

Brian laughed, too.

"Yeah, I wasn't sure either. I didn't want to assume."

This time, I kissed him. When we finally broke away from each other, I turned around to see Grace's math tutor staring at us.

"Mrs. Koncikowski," she said. "So nice to see you getting out." I turned beet red. I told Brian we needed to leave and he threw some money on the bar, grabbed my hand, and we ran laughing all the way to my car.

As I sat in his driveway fifteen minutes later, debating whether to follow him into the house, I texted Erin to give her the address, on the off chance he turned out to be a serial killer.

"Would you just enjoy yourself?" she texted back. "If I don't get all the details in the next two hours, I'll send the police." Brian's hands were around my waist and his mouth on mine as soon as I entered the house. During each room of the house tour, I lost a piece of clothing. As we made our way eventually to the bedroom, I whispered to him that it was just self-care and we both deserved to feel good. He looked tenderly at me as he pulled me towards him in the bed.

"Are you sure you want to do this?"

"I'm as ready as I can be and I'm glad it's with someone who gets it."

As I gathered my stuff up two hours later, I wondered what I was supposed to say now. *Was this it?*

"I had a really nice time with you tonight," he said and then continued, "Could we see each other again?"

I smiled slyly. "Do you like donuts with your coffee?" I asked.

"Yah, I do," he replied.

Before I had time to regret it, I blurted out, "I could probably get my Dad to come in the morning to watch the girls for a few hours. We could have donuts and coffee here if you like."

He chuckled. "Donuts and coffee, okay, I'd like that."

And so began my weekend mornings of visiting Brian's house with coffee and donuts in hand, to continue something like self-care.

After our third or fourth Saturday in bed, I had grown comfortable enough with him to linger a little longer. One morning after I stepped out of a shower together to towel off, he said something to me through the jet streams that sounded like, "This has been really nice but I'm just not sure I'm ready for a relationship."

I froze. *Oh God*, I thought. My stomach churned. Apparently, the sucker punch I felt upon hearing his words must have been linked to some kind of feeling I didn't know I had for him because I instantly felt rejected and panicky at the thought of being away from him. *Get your shit together Jeanette, do not cry in front of him,* I told myself. My brain went on high defense alert.

"Oh, um, okay. Do you want to talk about it or should we just stop here?" I asked. He got out of the shower, wrapped himself in a towel, took my hand and sat me down on the bed.

"It's just that I realize I'm really missing Leah and I don't know that it's fair to you that I'm all over the place with my feelings about this. I like you, and I don't want to hurt you but... I'm not really sure how to talk about it."

"Um, okay, sure," I said, as I got up and hurriedly threw on my clothes. *Do not cry, do NOT cry,* I told myself. As I put on my sneakers, I looked down at them and said to Brian, "So yeah, just call if you want to talk about it, okay. Thanks."

I couldn't get out of his house fast enough. The tears started streaming as soon as I pulled out of his driveway. I was mad at him, but mostly mad at myself. Turns out I was incapable of separating sex and emotions. In just the cumulative ten-fifteen hours we had spent together over a series of weekends, I found myself really caring for him. While I think we both tried to keep it light, we'd text every other day and talk on the phone once or twice during the week. While I wasn't ready to define whatever it was we were doing as a relationship, I definitely wasn't ready for it to be over.

I look back on that time and wonder why I felt the overwhelming need to be with another person so soon into my loss. Over and over on the widowed support groups online, people ask *How soon is too soon?* There is often a lot of judgment but that is counterbalanced by the sages who say, *Only you can decide when the time is right.* I wondered if the thought of navigating the days alone, with such troubling feelings and memories, could be lessened by the touch of someone new. For me, it had.

When I was with Brian, I could be both a grieving person and a new person who was having new experiences. I could get out of my head and my grief long enough to enjoy living in the present, even if that present moment only lasted as long as the orgasm did. I could also stop being a widowed parent and just be a woman again. A single woman, even. It didn't take long for me to realize that talking with someone other than Brian would not result in the same feelings. Since Brian and I had never agreed we were exclusive, I went back on the dating sites instead of talking to him. One guy I chatted with asked if I wanted to go to a naked boxing club together (Say what? Such a thing exists in Buffalo?) Another guy turned out to be the ex-husband of one of my good friends. We hadn't seen each other in ten years so we didn't recognize each other from our profiles. When he started talking to me about his ex-wife and how he was grieving her the same way I must be grieving my husband, I rolled my eyes, yet the particulars of his story sounded way too familiar. Sure enough, I figured it out. He still tried to go out with me as I reminded him that perhaps if he wanted women to take him seriously as a potential mate, he should try paying his child support bills to his first one. I switched my profile back to Woman-Seeking-Woman. Crickets.

I cried on Alice's couch in my weekly therapy session.

"It's okay to be sad about Brian. It sounds like you didn't know what you wanted from him until he started trying to figure out what it is he wants. Do we really know what Brian wants though?" She pushed me on the fact that I ran out of his house pretty quickly and hadn't responded to his calls or texts since then.

"Maybe he's right, Alice...maybe this is too much too soon for both of us," I bemoaned. And as Alice always did for me when I'd spin into relying on other people to take care of me, she brought me back to myself.

"What can you do for yourself right now, Jeanette?"

I paused my zeal for scouring the dating apps and went back to spending my nights ogling house profiles on Zillow instead. Whether my "situation-ship" (as I was calling it) with Brian was just a temporary escape from my grief or not, one thing was certain in my post-Mark life: it was time I figured out how to be alone.

Lessons Learned:
Post-Loss Sex or How to Get Comfortable Again
Getting Naked In Front of Someone New

Unless you've decided on a life of celibacy, sex will happen for you again. The timing matters less than how you approach it. Here are a few things I've learned since then about sex post-loss that might help lessen any burden you feel about it and increase the likelihood of enjoying intimacy with someone new.

1. **Get in touch with yourself first.** There was a period of time right after Mark died that even the thought of touching myself made me cry with longing for him. But just a few short months later, I was longing for some kind of adult-to-adult attention and affection. Before getting into bed with someone else, try getting in touch with yourself again first. When you can find self-pleasure again, it might be time to add in a partner.

2. **Make your peace with your deceased partner and the sex you had with that person.** Whether you like it or not, your partner is dead, and you are still alive and ticking. At some point, you are going to have to get used to the fact that they are not coming back and your sex life as you knew it with them is over. You will have to start over. For some people, this is harder than for others who had more sexual experience prior to their marriage or perhaps were in a non-monogamous marriage.

3. **Figure out what makes you feel safe about sex in the aftermath of your partner's death.** Do you need it to be with someone completely unknown to everyone else in your world? Do you need the comfort of an old friend or lover? Are you wanting to use this time to explore other sexual interests that you didn't or couldn't pursue in your marriage or life partnership? All of these things are fine. Thinking about what you want in a new person might go a long way in figuring out what your new boundaries are. Many widows and widowers with young children prefer a "friends with

benefits" situation in the beginning because they may not have the emotional energy or time to invest in a relationship. For others, their values may still revolve around sex occurring only in the context of a long-term relationship. Others still are happy being alone and having an occasional sexcapade when it comes into their life. What is it that would make you feel good given all that is happening in your life now?

4. **Look better, feel better?** I've never been a big proponent of the beauty industry's myths, but there is probably no time in your life you will ever look physically worse than when widowed. Grief ages us. We wear our sadness on our face and carry a heavy burden on our body. Plus, we're all snotty and bleary-eyed. We're lucky if we can get our kids showered and out the door, let alone ourselves. So, if you are getting ready to get some, make some time for caring for yourself in your quest for another. Retail therapy is a real thing. Get your hair done. Buy something sexy. Remember you are alive and as deserving of pleasure as anyone else.

5. **Be brave.** Say what you mean and mean what you say. Something happened when I was widowed. I lost my filter. I became the kind of person that no longer had time for social niceties. This both helped and hindered my quest for a new lover. Who you were in the "before" died the same day your spouse died. As the new you emerges, what does he/she/they want? Go get it. If you don't put yourself out there, it won't happen. Ask for what you want (in a husky bedroom voice even.) And check in with your new partner. Consent is sexy and a prerequisite.

6. **Enjoy it.** When the moment happens and you find yourself undressing for a new partner and touching them for the first time, breathe. Know the other person is probably as self-conscious as you are about their body and their story. Be honest about what you need. Take it as slow or as fast as you want. Cry if you need to cry. Call a friend for support afterwards. Enjoy it again.

7. **Remember, the best widowed sex is safe sex!** Don't go and get yourself an STD or unplanned pregnancy to worry about on top of all the other pressures in your life. Planned Parenthood is a good resource regardless of your gender, sexual orientation, or age. Be an adult and go get tested before and after as needed! Experiment with contraceptives and condoms until you find what works for you and your partner(s).

8. **Let go of the shame.** I've known more than one widow who has suffered from bacterial vaginosis after their first post-loss hookup. Their bodies, at a microscopic level, seem intent on making them feel bad about sex with someone new. It's as if their very own vagina is rejecting the idea. Sex post-loss isn't just about getting physically comfortable. You have to do the emotional work on yourself too, starting with any shame or guilt you're carrying into post-loss sex.

9. **Honor your humanity.** There is no shame in wanting sex after loss; whether two months, two years, or twenty years out. You decide the timeline and pace. You deserve affection, attention, respect and to feel loved and valued. You deserve pleasure. You deserve to live.

EIGHT

Surviving the First Year as a Family

In her book, *Second Firsts*, author Christina Rasmussen writes about the duality of how both everything changed, and everything remained the same after her husband died. "Nobody had warned me that I wouldn't be able to go back to what I had left behind."[11] But she also writes about the very practical ways in which the world continues to demand you stay the same. Widowed parenting demands we have to get up, feed our children, get them off to school and most likely return to doing whatever job we had before life as we know it changed. Widowed parenting is as much about moving in forward motion as it was in wanting to return to the past.

It turns out, there is another grief model that spoke to this feeling and experience of being pulled back-and-forth. It's called the Dual Process Model of Coping with Bereavement.[12] The Dual Processing model isn't about emotions. It doesn't talk about your anger, depression, or acceptance. It doesn't try to tell you how to feel. It simply categorizes your grief-related stress into two buckets: stresses related to what you lost or stresses related to what you are now being forced to rebuild after loss. The researchers who proposed the Dual Process

---

11 Christina Rasmussen, *Second Firsts: Live, Laugh, and Love Again* (Hay House, 1st edition, 2013), 4.
12 M. Stroebe and H.Schut. "The dual process model of coping with bereavement: Rationale and description," *Death Studies*, Volume 23, 197-224, 1999.

model believed that the movement between what was lost and what becomes restored is actually a healthy way to cope. It gives the grieving person just the right dosage of grief to be handled at any point in time, before allowing a break from that stress to focus on what is still ahead. And, unlike Elisabeth Kübler-Ross' five stages of grief model, the Dual Processing model has been studied and proven true over time and across cultures.

Thinking back on my first year after Mark's death, I can see how the Dual Process model of grief played out. I had to come to terms with the past, surrender to the present state of our lives, and still make decisions about our futures. I also saw how I was accomplishing some of William Worden's tasks of mourning. When I could step out and look at myself from a 360-degree view, I could see that I was changing far more than just our address. Somewhere during the year without him, I picked back up the work I had started when we separated. I was learning to live on my own, to trust myself, to tune into my intuition, and to be the sole decision-maker for me and the kids. My life had been reshuffled and I was still sorting out the cards, but I was starting to get more comfortable with not knowing what was next. Parents are not the only ones whose lives have been reshuffled though. Our children are facing a tremendous challenge to cope emotionally with their loss and to push through their day-to-day lives. Our biggest struggle may simply be to let what will be; be.

One night in late January 2015, about three months after Mark died and before the weekends with Brian, Grace said to me matter-of-factly, "It's Daddy's birthday soon, so we have to celebrate."

Veda nodded as if it was her job to be the eager sidekick and said, "Yes, yes. We have to have cake! And balloons. And sing Happy Birthday to Daddy!"

I excused myself from the table as I often did on the days I was overcome with emotion. I went into the bathroom, locked the door, and cried on the floor. This is what my children needed even if the thought of singing happy birthday to my dead husband made me incapable of standing straight. I knew I couldn't do it. I couldn't handle cake and candles. I asked myself, *what is the balance?* The girls wanted a ritual. It would have to be a new one. I wiped the tears as I had done so many times before, pulled myself up, splashed some cold water on my face and sat back down at the table.

"Girls, I've decided we should do something brand new for Daddy's birthday! I think we should show everyone how great your Daddy's heart was. What can we do to show people that?" As they picked at their chicken nuggets and mac-n-cheese, they suggested we could go to a water park in his honor. I chimed in that going to the water park was probably not a way to show people their daddy's big heart.

Grace looked at me. "I've got it! We'll do it like I do for the babies! We'll raise money and make someone's day better."

Grace had been having an annual lemonade stand to benefit a local hospital since she was six. I could live with a fundraiser. I didn't want Mark's birthday to be about how he died so instead of donating to an epilepsy-related charity, we decided to launch a virtual fundraiser and chose a charity that best reflected Mark's life. No charity had meant more to Mark in his life than the Society of St. Vincent dePaul, whose summer camp we had worked at as teenagers. As we snuggled into bed that night with my laptop between us, the girls helped me pick out camp photos and tell Mark's story as we created the virtual campaign. I called the camp the next day and found out it now cost about $400 a week to send a child to the camp. Most of the children who attended camp were there on church scholarships. I hoped we could raise enough to send one child to camp tuition-free. As the week crawled by, it was all the girls could talk about.

I spent the first half of Mark's birthday taking my own advice and doing self-care. I got a massage and then met up with my friends Amy and Erin. We all picked the girls up from school and went out to dinner at Mark's favorite Chinese restaurant. We ordered ALL the foods. Throughout the dinner, the girls would ask for my phone and refresh the fundraising app to see how much money had been raised. We were astonished as it moved from $500 to $1,000 to $1,500. Although they were young, both girls understood what camp and all it offered to those it served meant to Mark. They knew it was somewhere he loved and had good memories of. Both girls had spent their summers visiting this camp with us and even at their young ages, they seemed to understand the tangible benefits another child would have coming to this camp. Before we went to sleep that night, $2,500 had been raised.

"Look what we are accomplishing in your Daddy's name," I said as I kissed them both goodnight. I even found myself amazed at what had happened. I was so worried people were already forgetting Mark but instead, here they were, donating in his name. The next morning, I saw that a stranger had donated $500. The stranger was linked as a mutual friend of one of our friends from high school, so I reached out to her to see if she knew why they had been so generous. She immediately called me back and told me that she did not know the couple well, they were Facebook friends from her church. The wife had been looking at Facebook on her phone while her husband laid in a bed in hospice. She read our story on the link shared by this mutual friend and was so touched by it, she read it out loud to her husband when he awoke. He insisted she make the donation because, like us, they had worked at a summer youth camp when younger. It didn't matter that I didn't know them in person. I could feel their love and knew they felt my love for Mark. I also knew they were being touched by loss at that very moment. I was comforted by the knowledge that Mark's life would continue to affect other people. By the end of the week, we had raised $4,000; enough to send ten children to camp tuition-free. When I called the camp office to explain the donation, they asked whether I wanted to notify the families.

"No," I said, "just let them know that an angel took care of their tuition."

"Daddy would be so proud of us, wouldn't he?" said Grace. "Yes, baby, yes he would." We had made it through another first and came out better for it on the other side.

March and April brought a birthday for each of the girls. I did my best to make those days memorable, hoping they wouldn't feel the great big absence of their father at their birthday parties and equally afraid they wouldn't. The last party was a sleepover for Grace's school friends. Late that night, after all the girls were finally knocked out from sheer exhaustion, I poured myself a big ol' glass of wine and decided since I was already feeling pretty miserable, I might as well keep at it. I had made a commitment to getting the house on the market in the next two weeks. There were still boxes of Mark's things sitting on my porch that I hadn't touched. I opened a box that looked like it was filled with books, and right under the flap, as if meant for me to find it, was a book by one of Mark's favorite poets, the thirteenth century scholar and writer, Rumi. As I flipped through the book, always curious to see what Mark made of it, I saw his annotation. *The cure for pain is in the pain*, he had written alongside the same words by Rumi. His penmanship was impeccable, as always. I wondered if he had to write down the words he read so they sunk in. I had been doing everything I could to stop the pain. Sure, I'd let a little bit loose here and there, but I'd bottle it all back up after some of it escaped. I'd tuck it back into my pocket and go about my day, thinking I had accepted that Mark was gone. But when I looked up as my children blew out their birthday candles, I could see the imprint his absence left and at that moment, I couldn't accept it at all. I could only crumble.

Debbie Ford wrote in her book, *Spiritual Divorce*, these words about acceptance:

"Acceptance is the essential ingredient that enables us to begin the healing process...We cannot accept a situation until we're ready to look fearlessly at the facts of our circumstances."[13]

Ford suggests that when we practice acceptance, especially acceptance of the worst circumstances in our life, we harness a powerful, life-changing tool. It was one thing to decide to begin again. It was a whole other thing to accept the reality of Mark's death, of mine and the girls' loss, and all that it meant for our lives and then find the courage to take the steps to actually make a new life without Mark.

In each of the evenings that followed that week, I'd tuck the children in bed and then open another box of the life Mark left behind. As I went through one after the other, making decisions about what to keep and what to let go, I stopped trying to stop the pain. I cried. I wailed. When I had whittled the life he had led down to only two totes, four boxes of books, and a guitar, I was done. The tears stopped for now not because I was holding them in but because I had no more tears to cry. I'd needed my pendulum to swing to the past and hold tension there. Now it was ready for release again, as I shifted focus to our future.

---

13 Debbie Ford, *Spiritual Divorce: Divorce as a Catalyst for an Extraordinary Life* (Harper One Press, 2006). 13, 80.

The girls and I were spending all of our hours after school looking on the other side of town for the perfect little house for just us three. And we found it; and then lost it in a bidding war. This happened not once, but three times. Each time I got excited and wanted to share it with someone. The last time I called Brian. He said he was happy to hear from me. It had only been two, maybe three weeks, since I had fled his house.

"Please, can I see you?" he asked earnestly.

"I can't get a sitter until the weekend," I replied. He sounded disappointed, which made my cautious heart hopeful. "If you want to, you can come sit on the porch with me now. The kids are asleep."

Twenty minutes later, he was sitting on my stoop. It was the first time he had come to my home. I told him about how hard it had been to go through a lifetime of our belongings and whittle the remnants of the life Mark had led down to the essentials. One thing was sure about my move: the girls and I would be downsizing and a lot of things would have to go in the process. I asked Brian if he wanted to talk about his feelings about us in relation to his grief.

"I'm not very good with words like you are," he said, "But I'll try."

He explained how he felt judged when he told a friend he had been seeing someone; how much guilt he felt when he admitted to himself that he was developing feelings of some kind for me. What did it mean for his relationship with Leah, his wife, if he could move on so quickly? Leah had been gone for eight, almost nine months.

"It sounds like we've both been punishing ourselves," I said.

His eyes started to tear up.

"I just feel like I don't deserve to feel happy. She's gone and..." And I realized without him saying more what he meant. She's gone and he's still here. And just like I had been with Mark, Brian had been carrying around enormous guilt about Leah's death.

"You feel like it's your fault."

"Yes! It is my fault. I wasn't there for her!" His pain was audible in his voice. Brian then explained that Leah had passed away, overnight, in her hospital room. They had both expected she would be discharged the next day. Whatever

104

anger I had been carrying towards Brian because I felt rejected by him dissipated in that moment. He was as devastated and vulnerable as I was. Both of us were just trying to figure out how to get through this vast ocean of loss. I laid my head on his shoulder and took his hand.

"It's not your fault," I whispered over and over again, until he seemed to understand.

"Thank you for being here," was all he could reply. I kissed him before he left, and he asked if he could take me out on a proper date the following weekend.

"I'd like that," I said, and I meant it.

When we met again, it was at a cozy Thai restaurant and instead of focusing on our losses that night, we gave ourselves permission to just get to know a little more about the people we were before and the people we were hoping to still become.

A few weeks later, the house on Lake Avenue, the home that Mark and I had planned on raising our children in, sold to another young family. Just in time too, because I had found yet another "perfect little house." It was located on a tree-lined, child-filled street in the next village over. Same town. A fif-teen-minute ride away.

"It goes on the market tomorrow and I got you the first appointment of the day," said my realtor. I didn't really think I wanted to stay so close to our current house and neighborhood, but that morning, when I visited the little gingerbread-type cottage, I immediately felt like I had come home. The house was on a corner lot, with only a tiny backyard and small side lot. The yard looked overgrown and unkempt but when I stepped into the house, it was light and bright. The kitchen had been newly remodeled, as had the upstairs bath, but it retained charming vintage wood floors. It was 1400 square feet of move-in ready goodness. When I went outside to take a closer look at the yard, I noticed the tree near the bedroom that would be my own and it looked like a magnolia (my favorite kind of tree). And sitting high at the top was a big, black crow, Mark's favorite animal, squawking at me. I took it as a sign from Mark and I heard him whisper to me, *Welcome home, Jeanette.* I put in an immediate offer, and this time, it was accepted.

It was a fast sixty days. We packed boxes on the nights we didn't have appointments. Although moving day was a mad rush, the girls and I paused long enough to say good-bye to this house where we were last a family with Mark. I knew it was another watershed moment of their childhood and I wanted to honor that. I picked up a small bottle of bubbles and the girls and I went from room to room. "Tell me your favorite memory in this room."

After we laughed and cried, we blew bubbles all through the house, wishing nothing but goodness for the new family taking our place. It was hours later when we finally settled in for the first night in our new home. Grace was excited and wondered what their new school would be like. Veda refused to stay in her new bed. As she laid her little body against me, she was racked with sobs.

"Let yourself cry, baby. Let yourself get the pain out," was all I could muster.

Veda had been four when Mark and I separated; he died when she was five; and now at six, I was again turning her life upside down, moving her away from the only home she had ever known. As she cried herself to sleep that night, I prayed I hadn't made a mistake. It was the first night I questioned my decision-making since I had settled on selling the house in the first place. Once again, I heard Mark in my head, whispering to me that she just needed time. *The cure for the pain is in the pain. Do not try to fix it, Jeanette. Let her process it herself, in due time.*

The next morning, as I unpacked kitchen boxes, I watched Veda and Grace explore the new yard and tentatively exchange names and information with the children they saw playing across the street. Grace asked if she could go and play with the other children. I told her as long as I could see her through the kitchen window, she could go play in their front yard with them.

"Take your sister with you," I said to her.

"No," said Veda. "I hate it here. I'm going to stay here by myself."

"Okay," I said. "You can either come inside and help me or play on the side lawn where I can see you."

I watched Veda through the window, sad as could be. She picked up a stick and dragged it around. She threw some rocks at the big oak tree. She sat down on the sidewalk and curled into a ball. I resisted the urge to try to make it better. The phone rang and I was distracted for a minute or two. When I looked back through the window, I could see Grace running gleefully down the street with three other girls on bikes behind her, but Veda was nowhere in sight. I rushed outside and started calling for her. Silence. I ran to the back yard, all the way around the house and went back inside through each room. I started to feel frantic when I spotted her through the dining room window. She had climbed into the magnolia tree and managed to get herself up to a nice branch that held her in its cradle. She looked like she was singing softly to herself. I took a breath and went out to see how high she was. After convincing myself that she probably wouldn't break her neck if she fell, I went back inside to continue unpacking. Twenty minutes went by before she came in. I heard her run upstairs. She came bounding back downstairs, happy as could be now, with books, a basket, a Barbie doll, and ribbon in her hand. She asked me to make her a sandwich.

"What are you doing?" I asked.

"I'm going to live in my tree. When my sandwich is ready, you can put it in this basket that I will leave on the ground, and I'll pull it up there with me."

"Alrighty then," I said.

"Peanut butter and jelly?"

Ten minutes later, I watched her through the window, eating her sandwich and seemingly having a whole conversation with someone. When she came in again, I asked who she was talking to. She stared intensely at me before replying.

"I'm talking to Daddy, who is a crow now. You said so."

Sigh. I had to remind myself that children, like us adults, need to let their pain be spoken and be heard.

Grace and Veda promptly reminded me at the end of the first week in the new house that I had promised them a dog once we had a dog yard. It was as if they had access to the checklist in my head that read, "Our Life Post-Mark" and we were all checking boxes as quickly as we could. After a few Google searches for rescues near us, we made an appointment to go meet a dog named Charlie. Charlie peed on everything. Charlie was bitey. Charlie was not for us.

To console the girls, we stopped to get hot dogs (the irony). They dared me to eat a foot long and I did. Before we got home, I started to feel quite ill. Something hadn't agreed with me about the day. I needed to lay down. I called my father, telling him I must have gotten a bad case of food poisoning. I wasn't nauseous but something wasn't right. He came to take care of the kids and I fell into a deep sleep. When I awoke, I was feverish. My temperature was around 103 and it stayed there for almost a full week, despite medication. I struggled to take care of the girls and myself. I couldn't work and my father had to be with us every day and some nights. I saw my doctor on the fifth day, who told me it was likely just a bad viral infection. After seven days of the high fever, it finally dropped to around 101 and continued to linger there. I was also highly fatigued. I had never had a fever like this as an adult and probably not even as a child. I missed the wedding of a dear friend. I could only work from bed on my laptop. The girls fretted.

"You are not being very safe right now," Veda said solemnly to me.

"I'm fine, Veda. It's just the flu. I will be better soon."

Soon couldn't come soon enough, so on the tenth day, I drove myself to Urgent Care. More tests were run, checking for said flu and mono; everything came back normal. The doctor there noticed I had checked Widowed as my marital status.

"How long ago did you lose your partner?"

"Nine months ago," I said.

"What were you doing before the fever started?"

I proceeded to detail looking for a dog, the move, the clearing out of the old house, the clearing out of Mark's apartment, the clearing out of my heart.

"I see," the doctor said. "Your body is forcing you to slow down, whether you can admit that or not. Listen to your body. You need to stay in bed until the fever passes. You must let yourself rest. It has all been too much."

She marked my diagnosis as "Fever of Unknown Origin" and when I got the statement on the way out, it also listed "Grief - Prolonged."

It had all been too much. The doctor was not incorrect. My mind had been on hyperdrive since Mark died, with my body just along for the ride. I believe the term "whirling dervish" was an apt descriptor. Just when I thought I was starting to feel a bit more in control of my life again, my body gave up. This "fever of unknown origin" forced me to sleep more than I had in years. It forced me to lay still. It forced me to just be. I was not particularly good at just being. It was another four days before the fever finally abated. The exhaustion remained. The kids' growing demand resumed as soon as I seemed well enough. Each night, we went on Pets.com to look for the perfect mate to add to our brood. As if a new dog could replace the giant hole in our hearts.

So, when we took the hour-long trip down to a tiny rural village to meet Buddy, I wasn't expecting much. As we hesitantly went into a stranger's home and looked out into their yard, there was a little ball of blonde fire running circles around a pit bull.

"He's a mutt," said Buddy's foster mother. "Definitely part shih tzu and probably a terrier of some sort. He has a lot of energy but he's a bundle of love."

That bundle of love came indoors and then promptly jumped into Veda's lap and licked her face. I saw my child's smile come out and her inability to put it away. I hadn't seen Veda beam like that in almost a year.

Grace said, "We have to keep him, Mom!"

I didn't disagree. There was no better distraction than Buddy, who took their minds off the fact that they would be starting a new school the following week. Later that week, I realized Buddy was not in his assigned "getting-used-to-the-house" spot in the kitchen. I found him with his head lying on Veda's belly. She was crying and stroking him.

"What's wrong, V?"

"Daddy never lived in this house with us. I don't want to live in a house without Daddy. Buddy says he understands." Buddy shifted his eyes from Veda to me then, as if he really did understand our pain. I gave him a nice pat on the head.

"He's a good dog, I think." I said to Veda.

"Yeah, he gets me."

I laid down and held Veda as Buddy snuggled up close to us.

A few days later, it was time for school to start. Ever suspicious, Veda, now six, was none too happy about leaving me. To prepare her, I had met with the principal and her new teacher over the summer. I brought Veda in for a special tour of her new school where she had one-to-one time with both the principal and her new teacher. My child noticed another tree.

"There," she pointed. "You will stand there and wait for me every day. Promise me?"

I was too tired to argue, and I knew she felt safer with trees than people.

"OK, I will wait at 3:00 p.m. by this tree. And when you come out, I will give you a great big hug."

"You'll be waiting right here?" she asked again.

"Right here," I said. I fretted all that first day about how she would do. I kept my phone near in case the school called to tell me she couldn't handle it. But she did. As I made my way to the appointed tree at the end of the school day, I could see her little head peeking out the window, searching for me. Veda ran out of the building and jumped into my arms.

"See, I'm here at the tree. Tell me how school was!"

Veda proceeded to tell me all about her day and what she liked about it, what she didn't like about it, what she worried about and mostly how she just wanted to get home to check on Buddy. A few minutes later, Grace joined us and the three of us walked arm-in-arm to the new car which we drove to the new house in the new life we were rebuilding. As I watched them run down the street with Buddy later that afternoon, I tried to let it settle on me that we three were really going to be okay.

As with so much of my grief in that first year, I was okay until I was not okay. Our thirteenth wedding anniversary was approaching in the third week of September, and I let myself get pulled back under by the tide. I took the day off and went on a solo hike for a bit in the morning. Then I took some flowers to Mark's grave and felt the pain wash over me. The guilt came again; the sorrow came. I thought about what our life would have been like had he lived and we had divorced; what our life would have been like if he had lived and we had moved back in together. Neither of which we'd gotten the luxury to choose as death had its way with us instead.

The first anniversary of his death came six weeks later. It seemed impossible to me that a whole year had passed, and I knew that the night before the death anniversary would be the hardest for me. In true avoidance fashion, I booked myself a full day of work followed by a lecture I gave at my undergraduate alma mater. I arrived home late that evening. The children were already tucked into bed by my dad. When I came in to kiss them goodnight, I cried seeing their sweet little sleeping faces. Reflecting back on all the ways that the world had hurt them in the last year, I was also full of gratitude to be alive and together in this new safe space we had created.

As I tended to do, I again played the game of "What If" in my head. What if he had come home that night and had died with Veda in bed beside us? How much worse for the children's suffering and my own would that have been to be direct witnesses to his death? What if he had come home and I had been able to call 911 for medical attention? What if I hadn't talked myself out of calling and checking on him at 1:00 a.m.? In interrupting his sleep, could I have interrupted where his brain was about to go? What if he had a roommate? What if he had been consistently taking his medication? What if I had been the one to die in my sleep instead of him?

It's like the matrix—once you get sucked down into that dark place, it is hard to break out of the co-realities you can create for yourself and come back to the real one. I couldn't sleep until after the 3:00 a.m. hour had passed. The coroner believed he died sometime between 1 and 3:00 a.m. I went into my closet and took Mark's ashes out of their sacred spot in a suitcase. I hadn't decided what to do with this half of him yet. Despite Grace's initial suggestion that we spread them at the eternal flame at Mark's favorite park, I knew I just wasn't ready to let him go like that yet. I hugged the black box with his name and birth and death dates on it. As I laid in my bed alone that night, I went deeper and deeper into what his final moments must have been like. I sobbed until I felt the panic coming on and then I threw up. *This isn't any way to live, Jeanette. You can't change or control any of this now.*

Sitting with that knowledge on the bathroom floor, Mark's remaining ashes in a black plastic box next to me, I felt so powerless and so very sad. I dragged myself back into the bedroom, put the ashes on a shelf in the closet, and then must have finally slept.

The next day, I was grateful for a Halloween parade at the new school so the children had something to look forward to. I had the day off from both work and parenting to do some self-care. After dropping them off, I played the Guns and Roses trilogy we had loved when younger, drove to the cemetery alone and sat down next to his grave. I talked with Mark about all the ways in which I was struggling and asked him to send me a sign that he was alright on the other side. Immediately, a crow flew overhead, and I stopped crying. I looked around at the beauty of the cemetery on this cold October day and laid my hands on the stone, directing my energy to connect to whatever energy of his remained under the ground. I let the light wash over me and give me the strength I needed to get up and go about my day.

I'd be back later in the day with the children, but first I treated myself to a massage. Then Erin and Amy met me for lunch and a hike. We kicked around Mark's favorite park and I told them about my struggles to decide what to do with his ashes. Amy reminded me that Mark would send me the sign of what to do if I sat with it long enough and that there was no need to make any decisions just because a year had gone by. I gave myself permission: the ashes could stay in my closet for now. Gratitude again washed over me when the girls came out of school and saw Amy and Erin standing at the tree with me. They jumped into their arms and told them all about their day at school. Then the five of us went to our local grocery store to pick up flowers and small pumpkins to take to the cemetery together. We began our new ritual of writing love notes on the pumpkins to leave at Mark's gravesite and then, as we had done with his birthday, we went to his favorite Chinese restaurant and ordered his favorite foods. I reminded myself how not alone I was that day and how appreciative I was for these friends of ours who loved me enough in their loss of him to stay connected to us and even deepen the bond. We had survived the first year and, knowing we did that, we knew we would get through anything else.

The next night, I called Brian. I had appreciated the fact that he had given me space in the days leading up to the anniversary. We had been seeing each other exclusively since June. As the kids and I got into a more solid routine in the new house, sometimes Brian would come by after they had gone to sleep and sit out with me that summer on my patio. Now that I was working at home full-time, and he was too, we made the most of the days we could meet up for lunch. We hadn't labeled our relationship beyond agreeing that we wouldn't be seeing or sleeping with other people while we were together. I hadn't met any of his family or friends yet. He had met Amy and Erin, but that was as far into my life as I brought him. The children had no idea we were seeing each other for the summer and fall of 2015. They had met Brian once or twice at the Widow/er Meetup picnics or potlucks and we even drove him home once. He followed my lead. I planned to keep it that way a little longer because I didn't want to add another change to their lives. I went back and forth on whether to tell them, even going so far as to ask the almighty oracle.

I apparently didn't cover my tracks very well. One night, not too long before Christmas of 2015, Grace, Veda, and I were surfing the internet on my computer, compiling their Christmas list. I walked into the other room for a bit and came back in to hear, "Mommy! Why does this google search say, 'How to tell your children you are dating when widowed?'"

Shit. Veda stared intensely at me. Grace demanded to know if I was going on "hot dates." I responded, "Well, I've been thinking that it is time for me to think about going on a date sometime. We've talked about how hard it is to live without Daddy. It's hard for you two, and it's hard for me. Sometimes being an adult gets lonely and sometimes, I'd like to try to have some fun again in my life. Going out on a date with someone can be a way to do that."

Veda's stare grew more intent. "You can go out on a date with us if you get bored."

"Well, I appreciate that sentiment Veda, but sometimes, adults need time with other adults. To talk about boring adult stuff. Like banking. Or to go watch a hockey game."

Now Veda's stare turned to side-eye. My child knew me so well.

"You don't even like hockey," she said.

"Well, maybe I would if I went to a game sometime," I replied, thinking about the hockey tickets I was going to surprise Brian with as a birthday gift at the end of the month.

Grace butted in. "But who would you even go on a date with?"

"I don't know, people. You know, maybe a friend. Someone who is kind."

"Uh, huh..." said Grace. Feeling like they were getting overloaded on information, I decided that that was enough for one night and sent them off to get ready for bed.

I waited until they brought it up again, which didn't take long. That weekend, as we three walked back from our favorite breakfast place, Veda said, "Just so you know, I'll punch him."

"Punch who?" I asked.

"Anyone you date," was Veda's reply.

I stopped walking and got down to Veda's eye level. I explained to her that I loved her love for me and her love for her daddy. And that I would always love her daddy more than anything in the whole world besides the two of them. But when Mark died, I told her, the law no longer saw us as married and therefore, it's okay if I want to date someone else. And more importantly, I had been through a lot of pain, like they had, and I deserved to have someone take care of me and be nice to me and maybe take me out to a nice restaurant once in a while. None of those things would change the love I had for her or for her daddy.

"Fine," Veda said. "But I might still punch them."

Grace got philosophical about it. "I think it's okay, Mommy. You deserve to have fun because you are the serious rock. So, I say you can date someone, but you just can't marry anyone else, ok?"

I informed Grace that while I appreciated the support, my decision to start dating again would be my decision alone. I concluded with, "No one is trying to marry me, okay. Let's just take it one step at a time. I'll let you know if I decide to go on a date with someone and when I'm ready, you can meet that person, okay?" And then half-jokingly, "And no punching them, Veda. Because why?"

"Because hands are not for hitting," they squealed back, recalling a favorite board book from when they were younger and had to daily be reminded that it was not okay to slap, punch, or smack the other.

In an effort to help reassure the kids that we three were still a family, I decided it was time to get photos of us three up on our walls, alongside the pictures of all the people whom I loved that had passed. I set up a holiday family photo shoot and we even brought Buddy with us. As I hung the newly-framed photos in our dining room, Grace reminded me that one of her favorite Disney movies, *Lilo and Stitch*, is about a child who is orphaned and how Stitch says in the movie, "This is my family. I found it, all on my own. It is little, and broken, but still good."[14]

"Yes, Grace, our family is little now and maybe we still feel broken. But we are still good. And you two and that dog are goofballs!"

Every night after, when we sat down to dinner, the three of us stared back smiling and laughing. We are still good. I let myself feel that in my bones.

As that second Christmas without Mark approached, I walked into Brian's house and met his mother, father, and mother-in-law for the first time. He had told them he was seeing someone from the support group, and they had been pestering him for a while about when they would meet me. It was so hard for me to get time without the kids, so Christmas Eve day it was. As Brian and his parents did some work on the house, his mother-in-law sat with me at the kitchen table and said she was glad to meet me and that she could tell I was a good influence on him.

"He was so depressed after Leah died. We were all so worried about him," his mother-in-law said. I told her, without going too deep into the state of my marriage at the time, about Mark and how hard the last fourteen months had been on the kids and me. I told her Brian was a kind man and her daughter must have been special for him to love her so much. I wanted to reassure her that Leah was never far from Brian's mind or heart. We both cried.

---

14 Dean Deblois, Chris Sanders, Alan Silvestri, Mark Mckenzie Alan Silvestri, Tod Cooper, Tom Macdougall, William Ross, Mark Mckenzie, and Chris Boardman. Lilo & Stitch. USA, 2002.

That night, the girls and I started two new traditions that we have continued since. We chose a Christmas tree ornament to represent Mark for each year of his passing. As our first Christmas Eve truly alone approached, I wanted it to be marked less with sorrow this year and more in honor of all we had done to survive this first full year without him. One of the community traditions in our new village was for Santa Claus to parade through the streets on a fire truck on Christmas Eve. I wasn't sure how Veda would handle it, given her fear of sirens, and I was grateful when I saw the flashing lights approach without the sirens wailing. The kids ran out of the house and got their picture taken with Santa who gave them each a bag of candy. The village also encouraged the tradition of "lighting of the way" for Santa to return that night with his reindeer, so we brought out our candles in mason jars and placed them at the end of our drive-way. The new school also encouraged the kids to put "reindeer food" (oatmeal with glitter mixed in) down on the lawn so we sprinkled their baggies of reindeer food all over the lawn before we headed back inside. I felt Mark's spirit all around us that night and my sorrow was mingled with gratitude. A friend had sent me a copy of a poem called *The Four Candles*, which was a ritual for remembering a loved one and it reminded me of the four candles for advent. After our fun was done, I asked each child to get their favorite picture of Mark to put in the center of the advent wreath I had purchased. I then added our wedding picture and turned down all the lights. I told Grace and Veda we would remember Mark every Christmas Eve like this now, so his spirit could fill us, and his joy could carry us into the next day. As I lit the candles, I read the poem, by an anonymous author, tears running down my cheeks again.

Four Candles

The first candle represents our grief. The pain of losing you is intense. It reminds us of the depth of our love for you.

This second candle represents our courage. To confront our sorrow. To comfort each other. To change lives.

This third candle we light in your memory. For the time we laughed. The times we cried, the times we were angry with each other. The silly things you did. The caring and joy you gave us.

This fourth candle we light for our love. We light this candle so that your light will always shine. As we think of you each day and share your memory with our family and friends, we cherish the special place in our hearts that will always be reserved for you.

We thank you for the gift your loving brought to each of us. We love you. We remember you.[15]

The children held me tight and we three cried until our tears slowed. Then Grace asked if it was okay to get cookies for Santa, so we gathered a small tray of homemade cookies and milk for Santa and a bonus carrot for Rudolph. They left them under the tree. Then I tucked them into bed and came downstairs to have my peppermint cocoa alone and enjoy the peace of the evening until I was sure it was safe to start bringing out their gifts. I reflected on how, the year before, just six weeks after Mark's death, I couldn't stand to even be alone, my grief overwhelmed me so much. This year, I was holding it together and remembering him all at the same time. It was okay to feel the pain and to enjoy the holiday again.

The next day, the girls and I carried on our tradition of a matinee movie on Christmas Day and later that week, I gave Brian two tickets to an upcoming hockey game for his birthday. I told him about my conversation with the kids and asked how he felt about perhaps taking me on a "first" date to the hockey game. He could come over beforehand and say hello to the children. I told him they might interrogate him. He said he was ready.

In the weeks that followed, I mentioned to the kids as nonchalantly as possible that my friend Brian from the Meetup group had asked me on a date to a hockey game and I decided I was going to go with him. Much to my pleasure, Veda did not threaten immediate violence.

---

15 Anonymous, The Four Candles. Retrieved August 16, 2016.
URL: https://www.swanboroughfunerals.com.au/funeral-poem-four-candles/

"I see," was all she said. She then asked if Erin could babysit them that night so Erin could "check him out." I told the kids that they should be polite when Brian came to get me and that perhaps it would be a good time for them to ask him some questions to get to know him a bit. Grace asked if I liked him. I said I did.

"But do you *like like* him, Mom?"

"I *like like* him, Grace, but we are going take it slow and start here, okay?"

When he picked me up a few weeks later for the game, Brian came to the door with a bouquet of flowers for me. I brought him into the house as if it was his first time seeing the place and he and Erin pretended it was the first time they were meeting. While I felt a little guilt for lying to the kids about our relationship, I also reminded myself perhaps they didn't need the whole truth all at once. Let them digest this idea of seeing me with someone new. Erin gleefully took on the role of first date interrogator. *Where were we going? When would he have me home? What kind of car did he drive and where did he get his education?* She did so in such an overdramatic way that it was silly, and Veda and Grace joined in the silliness. They demanded to know whether he had any pets and whether he would eat nachos or popcorn at the game. Brian very kindly answered their questions and complimented Veda on her Star Wars shirt. I decided that was enough for one night and we left for the game. Later that night, we took a really sweet selfie together and both kind of looked at each other.

"It's too bad we can't share this with the world," he said.

"Why not?" I said, "My kids know now, and your family knows now. That was who was most important to us. I think maybe it's time we go fully public with this thing."

So that night before we left the game, we both posted the picture of us two in our jerseys at the hockey game. I introduced him to my social network as my "sweet bit of sunshine in the darkness." We both decided to change our marital status on Facebook to Widowed.

And that was that.

Lessons Learned:
Coping with Holidays, Birthdays, and Anniversaries

Holidays, wedding anniversaries, birthdays, death days, and other important dates that marked the passage of our loved one's life can be especially difficult days. The following considerations helped me; they may help you too:

1. **Be realistic about what you and your kids can and cannot do.**
    Accept that things will be different now. If you are struggling to do
    the things your children or family (or community) may expect you
    to do, seek help and explain why a task is difficult for you. Do the
    shopping online. Ask friends to help with gifts and cake. Go out to
    dinner or heat something up in the microwave.

2. **Hold your boundaries.** It's okay to say, *"not this year"* to invitations
    and expected holiday gatherings, weddings, baby showers, or other
    social events that feel like "too much." Seek out the people whom
    you feel closest to and give yourself permission to change plans.
    You do not owe anyone an explanation beyond, *"Thank you for your
    understanding but we just aren't up to it right now."*

3. **Indulge yourself.** Prioritize self-care on the hardest days. Skip
    work. Let your kids skip school (or send them to school so you get
    the day to yourself). Put the massage bill on the credit card. Listen
    to your needs and put them first.

4. **Create a new tradition or ritual when you have the mental and
    emotional space for it**. Remember your loved one and keep their
    spirits nearby marking their loss in your family traditions or rituals
    (when you are ready). These can be your old rituals, new rituals, or
    even blended-family rituals. There is no right or wrong way to mark
    the passage of these milestone days.

5. **Remember everyone in the family has feelings**. You are still a
    family unit and, as such, each family member will handle holidays
    and milestones differently, so touch base ahead of time with your
    kids to see what is comfortable for everyone as a remembrance or
    celebration (or ditching of such things if that feels better!). Most of
    all, be kind to yourself on these days.

NINE

Ripple Effect: Coping with Secondary Losses

One of the things that was unfathomable to me, until I lived through it, was the number of secondary losses that affected our family's well-being after Mark's death. Much like when a stone drops into the water and ripples out, the primary loss of our partner ripples through our families' lives in unexpected ways. Secondary losses include losses or changes we experience as negative to our relationships, our lifestyles, and our roles in family, community, and society as a whole. Examples of secondary losses include loss of attention, loss of self-efficacy, loss of a partner in activities, loss of faith, safety, and trust as well as loss of health and well-being. There is also loss of intimacy, loss of inside jokes and understanding, loss of identity, loss of social connections and loss of a planned future to contend with.[16]

I was shocked that by the second anniversary of his death, some of Mark's closest friends (as well as my own) were no longer in my life. Some of the people who had pledged to be there for me and the children at his wake were never heard from again. I felt the wound deepest from the friends who had been there with me the first weeks and months, clearing out his apartment, supporting us through the holidays—where were they now? Was it me or was it them? Or was

---

16 Brock and Pierce, *Parenting Through Grief: The Attenuation Approach* (Createspace Independent Publishing, 2014).

my grief and the person I had no choice to become simply too much for them to handle?

Christina Rasmussen speaks to this dynamic among adult friends in *Second Firsts*. She writes that she would have laughed out loud at you if you told her that most of her friends who were with her during the first year of her loss would be gone sooner than later. Most often this was not due to any clear conflict. It was simply that she became someone in her loss who was unrecognizable to her friends. The growth she had to do internally to cope with her loss permanently changed her and as a result, changed the relationships she had in her life at that time.[17]

Originally, when some of my own friends couldn't understand what I was going through, I turned to the widows and widowers I met in the Meetup group. But as I moved into my second year in the group, I found more differences than similarities emerge with them too. Most of the people in the group were twenty, thirty, forty and yes, even fifty years older than I was. Their struggles as a senior widowed person were so different from my own as a young, widowed parent. Still, for a time, I felt like I owed them a lot and I agreed to become their membership coordinator. Things went smoothly in this role until a gay man reached out to me about the loss of his partner. When I invited him to the group, some of the seniors in leadership positions lost their damn minds because they did not believe gay marriage, love, and loss was as valid and as equal to their own. So, I quit the group in protest, and Erika and Brian left with me. To compensate for this new loss, I started an online support group on Facebook for younger widowed parents, like myself. All families would be welcomed by my new Widowed Parent Project.

But no amount of emotional support could take away the very real pain I felt in my body now that Mark was not there to adjust, massage, or melt it away. Even when we were fighting, he would stop and help me if I developed a migraine. He'd rub the chronic pain I carried in my shoulders until I could move my arm again. As the wife of a chiropractor, I never had to pay someone else for this professional service. After his death, I couldn't afford to keep up

---

17 Christina Rasmussen, *Second Firsts: Live, Laugh, and Love Again* (Hay House, 1st edition, 2013), 86-87.

with the cost of three people getting monthly adjustments. In the early months and years when we did occasionally go to another chiropractor's office, the kids and I were often overwhelmed with sadness. These new chiropractors were not Mark. And we had to go there because he no longer existed to care for us or his patients.

I committed to continuing Sunday Fundays for the kids to address the secondary loss of playful and fun-loving Dad. I forced myself, even when depressed or overwhelmed with grief, to take the kids out for some kind of activity weekly that might just inspire a moment of joy or a laugh from them. In the beginning, these were often cost-free Fundays such as a hike in the park (which they still lament was not that fun despite the fact that as teens they both have a strong sense of environmental justice) or a spa day at home smearing banana on our face and mayo in our hair. When I could afford it, we went on bigger water park adventures for special occasions. I was hopelessly trying to prove to the kids and myself that Mark wasn't the only parent who could create fun memories.

Remember that big promotion I was up for the day Mark died? I turned it down when my company offered it several months later. The timing wasn't right for me and the kids. I needed the flexibility of working at home. But two years later, they asked again and this time, I took the promotion and the big boatload of responsibilities that came with it. I went from managing myself as a curriculum developer to managing a staff of fourteen. There was to be no more working at home. With the promotion and its associated pay increase, I could put the kids in before and after school care. But this meant we were gone from each other all day, every day. I was exhausted by the time dinner was finally made and worse yet, I had to work in the evenings at home. The long-term implication of a future where I was solely responsible for putting two kids through college outweighed the short-term needs of my kids, two years out from their father's death, for more time with their mother. That was the trade-off I made in my mind. As a professional, I have never regretted the decision to take the executive management position. But as a solo parent, I sure did.

My extended workday seemed to be felt the hardest by the children when Mark's absence was most notable at school. The little house we moved into was in a more affluent neighborhood than where Mark and I had lived. It cost me everything I had left to get us in that house, but it also came with associated social costs. We now lived in a school district where it seemed I was often the only single parent in the classroom. There were endless numbers of stay-at-home moms and even some stay-at-home dads. Parent Teacher Association (PTA) meetings were made with those people in mind. So were class field trips. It was at the end of Grace's first year at the new school when she pointed out to me that I had never been "homeroom mom" or chaperoned a field trip. To do so, I'd have to take another day off work to attend mandatory parent volunteer training. The privilege of the two-parent family was strong in our district and the expectations were there not only from my kids, but from the other parents I was trying to befriend to make up for all those other people who had stepped out of my life. I constantly felt like I was failing someone: my boss, my writing deadlines, one or both of the kids, the PTA moms, the teachers. After that first year, I accepted that it was not possible for me to work the hours I worked in the job I did and excelled at AND be the amazing school mom/cheerleader. I made it a point to not change out of my power suit when I showed up late for school meetings. And if I couldn't get to the fourth musical recital of the year, my dad went instead. I made sure that I did sign up at the start of the next school year for one field trip per kid but never did become a "homeroom mom." My time as a member of the PTA was short lived because it turns out those same stay-at-home moms who make a career out of the PTA positions had no interest in accommodating moms like me. I accepted all of these things as the trade off to my kids getting a top-notch education and living in a more child-friendly neighborhood. Someday, I hope my children will understand the sacrifices I made were done for consideration not just of their short-term needs, but of their long-term needs, as well.

Just like I struggled to find my place within our new school community, there were times they did, too. When you bear direct witness to your children's grief, to all the primary, secondary, and even tertiary losses, you can't help but want to do all you can to protect them. One of the hardest days for Veda and me that first year at the new school was when Father's Day rolled around. Every other child in her classroom had a living father who somehow was not needed at work that morning so they could attend the Dad and Donuts sing-along and celebration in the first grade. I anticipated the school would probably do some kind of sentimental thing involving food to mark the day like they had with Moms and Muffins for Mother's Day. Shortly after that lost morning at the office, I emailed Veda's teacher to ask about Father's Day, reminding her that Veda's father was deceased. She suggested that either I come or perhaps one of Veda's grandfathers could come instead. I called her the next day.

"I don't think you understand my point, though." I gritted my teeth and said, "You want my kid to stand on stage and sing along about how great dads are when her father will not be in the audience because, again, he's dead. And then when the dads walk across the stage, Veda has to experience, once again, being different and then having all of these people wonder why my kid doesn't have a father here. I'm not going to have my child participate in that as if she should just go along with it to keep up with her peers." The teacher didn't have much to offer as an alternative, insisting Veda would be okay. After determining that there was really no alternative that would work to meet my child's antici-pated needs, I decided to pull Veda from school for the concert.

Secondary losses generally have to be dealt with when they come up, which usually means at inconvenient times. While it's not always necessary to "process" everything with your kids at the moment something happens, it can be good to check in with them if you notice the impact, name the expe-rience, and offer support in coping with them. To help Veda cope with being pulled out of school so she didn't have to knuckle through Dads and Donuts Day, my father came and took her out for a special breakfast with just the two of them instead.

Like with primary losses, we cope with secondary losses by acknowledging the pain they cause in our minds, hearts, and bodies. After the first year without Mark, whenever I felt I was "sucker punched by grief" and something caught me off guard, it was usually a secondary loss I had not anticipated. One way to minimize the impact of secondary losses is finding alternatives, whether for role fulfillment or meaning-making. When I got the promotion and could no longer work at home, one of the first things that went was the state of cleanliness of the house. With the extra income, in addition to putting the children in before/ after school care, I also hired a housecleaning service. This is an example of finding an alternative for role fulfillment. We also joined a support group for children and parents who were bereaved, offered through our local grief counseling center. It was in this group that my children met other kids who were grieving. For the first time, they didn't have to pretend as they did with their other peers that everything was okay.

Lessons Learned:
Finding New Social Connections for You and Your Kids

We lose more than we expect to after our partner dies. While it is important to acknowledge secondary losses and feel the associated feelings, you can reengage the world when you are ready by actively seeking new experiences and new people to meet your family's needs. Making new friends as an adult is hard. Dating as a widowed person is hard. Changing your kids' home or school is hard. Helping your children connect to a stepparent is hard. But these may all be part of the work of healing our grief. Here are some things I did to help myself and the kids find a new social scene. I hope some of them work for you, too.

1. **Tune into your interests and search for like-minded folks.** While there were only two other widowed parents in the Widow/er Meetup group in my local area, I invested in getting to know both of these moms and their children and made time to socialize with them. I needed to be with other parents who "got it" and the children did, too. When it was hard to find sitters to get out of the house, I capitalized on the bevy of opportunities to connect to interest groups online. I joined and started engaging with online garden groups, widowed parenting support groups, and even took an online cooking class without having to ever leave my home. Volunteering and community service are also a great way for your children to get perspective on the hardships in their own life.

2. **Try new experiences; say "yes" more often.** Go to the theater with the extra ticket from a mom at your kids' school. Say yes to the weekend playdate. Go on one date to see how your body and mind feel about the prospect of someone, anyone, new in your life. Just be careful not to overextend yourself and take on too much at once.

3. **Know what your kids need.** Siblings will grieve their loss differently depending on their ages, development, personality, closeness to their parent, etc. Find and support your children in the activities they want to pursue to help them fill the void and gain new

experiences and skills. Grace happily attended three years in a row of grief camp. Veda, however, would not leave my side. So, after Grace came home and told us about the activities she was doing at camp, Veda and I recreated one of the art projects in our own "class" at the dining room table.

4. **Don't wait for offers of help; ask for it.** Sometimes, within weeks of your loved one dying, the social support that was there dries up. When you are a few years out, no one offers anything. Try being proactive when you feel least like doing so. Call your aunt and ask her to babysit on Saturday so you can attend that lecture at the university you want to hear. Go through your contacts list and text a friend you haven't talked to in a while. See if they want to meet up with you for a hike or a drink after work. Find out if your sitter can come an hour earlier once a week to give you time to exercise with a work buddy. Get comfortable stating your needs to others and accept what support they can offer. You might be surprised by the people who come into your life and offer a great friendship when you least expect it.

5. **Think before you date.** When you are ready to start dating, be honest with yourself about what you want that to ideally look like. When will you find the time? What will you sacrifice? How comfortable are you bringing someone home and when is the right time for your kids to know about a new special someone? While every widowed person has their own timeline, I do strongly recommend you assess how your kids will feel if they find out you are seeing someone and how their lives will change if you bring that person into their lives. Even older teens may struggle with this. Pay attention to your intuition and whether your new person is going to be comfortable not just being in your life, but being in your kids' lives too. Be ready to shift gears if your kids need time to adjust.

TEN

Solo Parenting: Impact on Body, Mind, and Spirit

It seemed to me that the stronger I got emotionally and mentally at coping with Mark's death, the more my body broke down. Early in the new year of 2016, while boxing with Joe, he noticed that I was holding my arm and then shaking it off when I threw a right hook.

"What's up with that?" he asked.

"I don't know, I think I did something to it."

Joe suggested I get a doctor to check it out. I still hadn't seen a rheumatologist like I should have after my finger had turned blue, but I had finally gotten myself on a waiting list and the appointment was coming up. When I did see the doctor, she did some testing of my shoulder and promptly sent me for an MRI. She told me to take a break from boxing until we determined if I had torn my rotator cuff. When the MRI came back, it showed I had bursitis, or assumed temporary inflammation of the joint. I took a break from boxing for a few months. It wasn't long before I started having pain in my wrists, too, and then my fingers began to ache. Over the next three months, I saw a carpal tunnel specialist, a spinal doctor, and a neurologist. My muscles constantly ached. My shoulder felt like someone was stabbing me in the back blade. My hands were swelling on a regular basis, and I had migraines that knocked me out for hours at a time. When I was at my worst, I'd have to call my dad or a friend to come over to take care of the kids. Then the pain and swelling started in my ankles. I grew increasingly anxious about my health and started to voice the nagging thought I had in my head since all the other losses: I was next in line to die.

It turned out that I had two herniated discs in my neck, which could account for the shoulder blade pain, the carpal tunnel pain, the finger aches, and also the migraines. The spine specialist said unless I wanted to consider surgery, which I promptly vetoed because that seemed terrifying, I was going to need to get some physical therapy. I was also to stop all activities that created more pressure on my neck and joints, specifically those high impact loves of mine: boxing and horseback riding. I cried when I left her office. Boxing and riding were the two things I did for me. They were where I went for time to think, for solace, or for time not to think and to just be in my body. Barnaby, the beautiful Clydesdale who had been my sidekick on and off for the last three years, was to no longer be a regular part of my life in the after-Mark. I called Beth first and told her the bad news. Then I called my boxing instructor, Joe. Both of them said they'd take me back as a student whenever I felt up to it.

Once I was back at the rheumatologist's office, she looked over all the imaging and the continued swelling of my hands and feet alongside the skin flaking off my fingers and decided I also had psoriatic arthritis. "Probably fibromyalgia too," she stated plainly. She loaded me up with a bevy of nerve medications on the way out the door after I refused to be put on heavier biologic medications that included cancer as a "rare but serious" side effect. I already had a high enough risk of breast cancer and cancer had already killed three people I loved. No way.

Two weeks on the medication regimen and I could barely take care of the kids. I felt high all day long. I was afraid to drive them anywhere. I had taken to walking to school with them even though I was hurting. These new diagnoses were not going to work with my solo parenting lifestyle. I called the doctor to ask how to stop the meds and then promptly switched rheumatologists. The next doctor got me in within a few weeks but after reviewing all the films and CDs and sad history I brought with me, she didn't have much better news for me.

"If you don't reconsider taking biologics, you're going to be in a wheelchair before 50."

I left with a script for a different nerve block and a low-dose antidepressant that was supposed to help me sleep so my muscles could repair themselves at night. I quit the antidepressant on the second night because it made me feel like my heart was going to explode. The nerve block didn't touch the pain. A few weeks after that, with the pain consuming every twist and turn of my body, I agreed to try an immune-suppressing drug. I took the first dose at bedtime, and, in the morning, shortly after I arrived at work, I started bleeding heavily even though my period wasn't due. I bled so much that I worried I was pregnant and miscarrying. A co-worker drove me to the emergency room where I waited five hours to even be seen by a doctor. By the time a doctor finally examined me, the bleeding had slowed. No pregnancy was detected so he thought perhaps I was having an adverse reaction to the medication and suggested I stop it immediately. Then another drug was prescribed by the doctor and with it, another trip to the ER, this time for an allergic reaction. My immune system seemed to hate me.

I had been on and off nine different medications by this point and was starting to feel like I would never solve this puzzle. I switched rheumatologists again and, this time, I found one who offered both holistic care alongside traditional western medicine. I found one who actually listened to my entire story and symptoms; who didn't simply assume that losing my husband was causing my hysteria.

After taking in everything I told her, she said, "So you had a fever when your symptoms started, and it went on for more than a week? Have you been tested for mono or parvo virus?"

I told her my last rheumatologist tested for mono and rheumatoid factors when I started with her and both tests were negative. I had never heard of parvo virus and didn't remember discussing it with any of my providers, so she suggested we get some blood work as a baseline and go from there. She explained that the virus can cause an inflammatory response that impacts your joints and mimics arthritis.

At the follow-up appointment, the new doctor informed me that the bloodwork had confirmed her suspicions. Her hypothesis after looking at the old X-rays I brought of my hands and neck were that I probably already had mild psoriatic arthritis before Mark had died. She suggested that the stress of his death and all the stressors faced since may have been what initially flared my hands and migraines but then I must have gotten the parvovirus when I fell ill with the fever that past fall, and as typical for its pattern of disease, the joint impact began and spread throughout my body in the months that followed.

"The good news and the bad news is that it's inflammatory. Because it's a virus, it should eventually leave your body but for some people, it can take ten to fifteen years to fully recover." I couldn't decide if I should cry in relief or cry because I couldn't imagine another decade like this. The doctor explained that she didn't think I'd see significant joint progression, the kind that would land me in a wheelchair as the doctor before her had predicted. She also said there was no treatment that would resolve the course of the illness because it was viral, which explained why none of the medications I had tried had made things any better. She said the best thing I could do for myself was treat the symptoms through physical therapy, acupuncture, massage, chiropractic treatments and when those weren't enough, steroids and anti-inflammatory medications.

Losing your spouse is one of the most stressful things that someone can go through and the limited research out there on widowed parents has found they encounter even more stress than our older widowed peers without children. Specifically, younger widows and widowers have been found to have higher levels of grief and depression than their older counterparts.[18] Quite simply, losing your partner and parent of your children in your twenties, thirties, forties, or early fifties can wreck your life. It disrupts not only our present, but our expected life trajectory. Our future becomes unimaginable. Then pile on the daily toll of solo parenting, including the emotional and financial stresses that

---

18 L.E. Amster and H.H. Krauss, "The relationship between life crises and mental deterioration in old age," *The International Journal of Aging & Human Development*, 5(1), (1974): 51–55, https://doi.org/10.2190/JA32-3VFR-29X4-D3Q7

come with it, plus a heap of social isolation, and it's no wonder that our physical and mental health suffers so. Our health is also directly impacted by our outlook and our access to support. In his book, *The Body Keeps the Score*, Dr. Bessel van der Kolk writes:

> *Traumatized people do not recognize their bodies as a source of pleasure and comfort or even as part of themselves that needs care and nurturance. When we cannot rely on our body to signal safety or warning and instead feel chronically overwhelmed by physical stirrings, we lose the capacity to feel at home in our own skin and, by extension, the whole world.*[19]

Maybe the doctors were right to be concerned about the impact of all this stress. Certainly, as my physical health became progressively worse in the two years after Mark died, my body remained heavily on guard. I was convinced in my bones and in my cells that the grim reaper was coming for me, too. I read *The Body Keeps the Score* again during this time in my life, trying to let the idea that trauma resides inside the body settle on me and taking Van der Kolk's advice to try to befriend my body and notice its flow of sensations, panic, uptightness, and impulses. I would need to learn to listen to my body. Set limits on who and what I would allow to influence me. Befriend myself and my fears. In those days, though, I couldn't shake this belief that my death clock, too, was ticking. I desperately needed to know I was going to survive this. That's all I wanted. To survive. Thriving hadn't really even crossed my mind at that point in time.

In those rare moments when I could calm my mind and as a result, quell the uprising in my body, I felt a deep connection to Mark. I carried his voice inside of me and sometimes it was so real, I began to wonder if I was experiencing a spiritual occurrence or just more evidence that I was losing my damn mind as days in the after-Mark era turned into weeks turned into months and then, somehow, two years. I rationalized that if death was coming for me, too, perhaps it was time to start paying my spiritual growth more attention.

---

19 Melaragno, "Trauma in the Body," 2018.

Google, my trusty sidekick, informed me that hearing voices from spirit had a name: clairaudience. What if Mark really was there with me this whole time? Giving me strength when I felt most broken. Prompting me forward when I was too scared to make a decision. It was either that or accept that I was hallucinating. I had returned to churchgoing during this time, and it was at Sunday service where I regularly heard and felt Mark.

The children and I would walk up to our little blue church in the new village as another part of our "new life schedule." Joining the Unitarian Universalist congregation gave me respite on Sundays for a sacred hour. The kids could go down in the church basement to craft during the sermon and I could sit for at least half an hour with my thoughts, present in my body, feet on the ground, watching the light and shadows of the stained-glass bounce around the room. Sometimes, during singing, I could feel the light swell and wash over me. I'd be flooded with the good memories of my time with Mark and let myself revel in those.

Reconnecting to my spiritual self only strengthened my interest in answering the question of where was Mark now? What happened to his spirit when his body died? Why and how had he died? Why didn't he fight harder to stay with us? Could he forgive me for leaving him and letting him die alone? When would I stop feeling this overwhelming anguish? And was it possible that he was communicating with me, to let me know, when I was able to quiet, that he was still there with me? Like a drum beating in my heart, its pounding got louder and louder as I approached the second anniversary of his death. I needed peace and I needed absolution.

Just about an hour outside of Buffalo is Lily Dale, a community of spiritualists, based in one of the more rural parts of Western New York, nearing the Pennsylvania border. Most Buffalonians know of this quirky little town and every summer, the spiritualists there open it to the public for mediumship, psychic readings, tarot cards, and more. I had never gone but had always been intrigued by the idea of a secluded group of "crazies" (as my father called them) living life in connection to the other side. While I usually let the intellectual, skeptical part of me reign supreme, Mark's death had awakened a need in another part of me to know more.

After talking through the pros and cons of a mediumship visit to Lily Dale with Erin and other friends at length, we figured the worst that could happen was that I was conned out of $200 or perhaps, given false information that made me question Mark's love for me. I could handle that. I decided to approach the quest for a spiritual experience in Lily Dale as just that. A quest. There were probably over fifty mediums at Lily Dale and the best lived there year-round, continuing to see seekers during the off-season. After reading countless reviews, I booked an appointment with one of the mediums who had the highest ratings. She billed herself as a second generation Lily Dale medium. I gave her no information besides my name and (gulp) credit card number.

I knew that whatever the experience was at Lily Dale, it was likely going to make me emotional, so I asked Erin to tag alone. She was down for the ride. It was a beautiful fall day, and the drive was scenic. Pulling through the gates to Lily Dale really was like an experience from a Grimm's fairytale. It looked like a ghost town. Falling down Victorian houses abounded. Hand-painted signs directed us to the fairy path or the Forest Temple. No one was on the streets. There were rustling leaves on ancient trees. We found a parking lot and got out to explore this psychic village, since we had a whole hour yet before I was to meet Nell, the medium. As Erin and I played through the magical paths in the woods and shopped at the heavily-incensed bookstore, I grew more and more skeptical. It seemed like an adult amusement park and soon the charlatan would appear to take my money. Erin left me on the porch of a little blue house with a white wicker couch where a sign instructed me to wait until called in. The minutes passed slowly until the door opened and a beaming woman with tears streaming down her face, emerged. She kept hugging the woman who I knew from her website to be Nell.

Nell was surprisingly younger than I thought she'd be. She greeted me with a warm hello and I was immediately captivated by her. She exuded warmth and light, in an almost celestial way. I felt the skeptic knock hard on my head. *Brace yourself, Jeanette, this is probably all bullshit,* I thought. Nell ushered me into a front room that looked a lot like any therapist's office would. There was a table-top water fountain running and soft meditative music in the background. Nell explained how the reading would work. She invited me to hold her hands and take a few deep breaths to center ourselves as we started. She then said a prayer, asking my loved ones to come to me in my time of need. We opened our eyes and she said nothing for what felt like a really long minute.

Finally, Nell took a breath and told me that the first spirit guide coming through was a rotund older lady with white hair, a big belly, and a warm laugh. *Grandma Doyle*, I thought to myself. My mother's mother had passed a year and a half after my mother died, the January before Mark's October death. Most everyone my age has a dead grandma that was overweight, so nothing too special here, I observed. But still, I replied to Nell. "It could be my grandmother." Nell's next statement surprised me. "She's showing me her white sneakers, like tennis shoes, does that mean anything to you?" OK, that's interesting. My grandmother was a waitress for thirty-five years. She wore white sneakers and a white apron to work every day. Nell probably googled me and would have found the obituaries for my mom, Mark, and my grandmother even. Lots of waitresses' wear tennis shoes, I thought. Nell continued that my grandmother knew I was dealing with a lot of "financial wrangling energy" and that I had been off work for an extended period of time, trying to get something squared away. She said my grandmother knew my mother was nearby. I held my breath. Nell described my mother as still dealing with anger and feeling catty with others. She said I had learned not to do that. To not be like my mother in that way. The skeptic in me thought, *clearly Nell doesn't know my mother as my mother was kind to all.* Then I quietly noted to myself that my mother never dealt with her anger about anything. She acted like it was an emotion that just didn't exist, even though on occasion I could see it flash through her quickly. Catty though? Nell must be picking up someone else's mother.

"Your grandmother wants you to take the time to feel a connection with God. You need to know that there is no illusion of separation from the divine. Lean on God; pray and lean upon God. And lean upon your grandmother, call on her spirit because she loved you. She taught you how to give grace and how to give love. She says, 'this too shall pass.' That you tend to get mired down. So do your children."

Tears started quietly welling. Nell continued in her calming, soothing tone. I sat up now, wiping the tears with my sleeve, most curious as to what my dead grandmother would say about my children.

"The little one is hypersensitive; amazingly resilient, both of your girls."

How did she know I had two girls? The obituaries again maybe?

"Be careful with the little one," Nell warned. She told me that Veda was the type of child who wanted to disappear. That there was a shy part that was strong in her. Nell continued, "While she's not painfully shy, she has a tendency to shut down in anger and she'll go through periods as she ages now where she'll struggle to find her voice, choosing instead to shut down and be angry, until she can find her voice."

Well, that does sound like my child.

"Once she finds it," Nell said with a smile, "she won't have to yell to be heard or be obnoxious to her sister." She then proceeded to tell me that my other child had "a big chip on her shoulder" because of her father. Her father wasn't making himself available to her and she's still mad about that. I straightened up. *Was this it? What would Nell share about Mark?* The next words out of her mouth dropped my jaw. Nell closed her eyes and put her hands over her heart. Her face seemed thoughtful and then saddened.

"He had a brush with death before his passing, yes? There's a feeling of pressure on my chest. A slam. A near miss."

My eyes widened. She knew he was gone and now she was describing something I was sure no one else knew about Mark but me and one other person. Two or three weeks before he died, Mark had been out running late at night and had been hit by a car when it rolled through a stop sign. The car struck him hard enough for him to fall to the ground, but he refused to go to the hospital, even though he had bruises on his chest and chest pain. I gasped; how could she know this?

Nell continued to share that she could tell Mark also had "a problem with addiction energies." She said that medication energy was trying to help him with "mental stuff." She laughed then. She said, "Grandma tells me he was wonky and needed it. He had a really skewed version of the world. But you stuck by him through this horrible, wacky stuff."

Nell went on to describe Mark as another big kid I had to take care of. She even went so far as to say that it was a blessing to have had him pass; to not have to worry about who he was going to be when he was home or whether he would be safe around us. She looked at me perplexed then, as I sat there, now sobbing in the chair, and shaking my head back and forth at such a suggestion.

"He had major issues," she said softly. "Some of this is above and beyond the call of duty. He had deeply rooted issues and it all fell to your shoulders. Grandma says one more thing. You need to tread lightly with your oldest, she noticed his depression. She wants to keep her dad on a pedestal, but she noticed it."

"Please! Please, is he there? Can I talk to him?" I implored Nell. She sat back and took a long breath. "He's working through his life review." Nell explained that when people pass, they have to spend time reviewing the good, the bad, and the ugly of their lives and look at lessons learned. They have to examine how their behavior affected others. She said Mark's passing hadn't been that long in the grand scheme of things and that his spirit felt somewhat removed to her because of this. She paused and looked around the room. "Grandmother is going to help him; she will try."

Nell then spoke about my anxieties and how I had to be careful not to transfer them to the children. By this point, I felt like she was an old friend who was reading my mind. I was crying deeper than I had in months; letting myself fall apart in front of this woman whom I was sure was used to being a comforter. Nell firmly took my hands in hers and looked me in the eyes.

"You cannot dwell on this. You have to move forward. You keep second guessing yourself, but you were not wrong. Trust your intuition. He knew how to emotionally blackmail you and he could spin it all. But you were not wrong. You must let go of the woulda, coulda, shoulda's, do you understand?"

"Please, Mark, please…if you are there, please come to me now," I begged.

And like a scene straight out of the movie *Ghost*, I felt Mark's presence in Nell. Her tone shifted with me again. Nell stated firmly that Mark did love me, as much as he knew how.

"He's not good at the being-in-the-trenches love, at the everyday love." She huffed, "You could have made him work for it more." Then she softened as she said, "He knows you love him, but you feel so guilty. The guilt outweighs the time you can feel the love energy. This was not your fault. It wasn't your job to be his keeper. He knows you're sorry for what you did. And he's sorry too. He realizes now he took so much out on you—his frustrations with his family, his feeling not rewarded at work, he was so handicapped by his own dark mind. With all of this, he realizes he did think in ways that weren't healthy. At many points, he didn't even believe in God, and he realizes how absolutely ridiculous that was. He's had his comeuppance, let me tell you!"

She looked around the room.

"He's teasing you, that you like all that new-agey stuff. Tarot cards and angels." She continued telling me about all of Mark's collections of books and his love of music. "So much music!" she exclaimed.

We joked that he must have been spending all of his heavenly time at concerts.

"And he left you with so much stuff to go through. Oodles! Oh, and he wants you to know you did the services beautifully. He says he didn't deserve all of that."

She explained that Mark wants me to make sure my brother gets acknowledged. For what, I wonder? And before I could ask, she said, "For being there when you were a puddle and you needed somebody to stand up for you."

I thought back to the first two days after Mark's death, when I had to make decisions at the cemetery.

"Everything rubbed you raw with grief." *How*, I wondered, *how could this be real?* Nell's voice softened even further, and she took a deep breath and sighed.

"You two were so unhappy for so long. He realizes now that you wish you could have escaped the relationship and maybe if you had, you wouldn't be feeling so bad now. He knows you stayed because you are loyal and loving and faithful, and you don't like to quit."

Nell looked to her left and said, "Grandma says he's going to be a much better boy now. She also knows you don't like to fail and she doesn't want you to look at this as a failure. A lot of this was his decision."

As if in a confessional, I told Nell of the sins I believed I committed in my years loving Mark imperfectly. The ways I deserved blame for the breakdown of our marriage especially. The ways I felt I had failed him, our children. and even myself. I knew this would be the only time I could get these answers, so I stammered out the words to Nell, "Was he alone, alone and in pain, when he died?"

I started to shake and cry harder, rocking myself now in an attempt to self-soothe.

"Shhh…" she said, a smile widening on her face. "No one is ever alone," she replied, handing me more tissues. "Angels gathered around him. He says he didn't have people with him when it was time, but he knew this was it. You see, death is between the individual soul and God. He said he didn't know what else to do. And he had turned away from God. He did this out of his own selfish pity. And he's sorry that people, that you, found him that way. It was horrible. And selfish and self-pitying."

My body was racked with sobs, recalling those first moments of finding him on the floor and trying to save him. All I could mutter through my tears was, "I tried, I tried to save him. I tried to save him, but it was too late."

Nell's voice got even softer. "You put up with a lot of abuse. And you didn't tell your friends or family. You kept it all inside of you and let that pain eat at you. You don't have to do that anymore. What you're going through now, with your health, is the physical response of having to hang on to the burden of private things."

I hadn't mentioned my health issues to Nell at all, but clearly, she and Dead Mark knew all about them. Nell then took on the role of cheerleader, telling me with great enthusiasm that it was time to get myself focused on healing. She said I could continue to be the steadying force for my family but that it was imperative I focus on self-care. And not "pretend self-care" but real self-care. She said I had to let my friends help me.

"He says to say hi to the one who came with you today. He appreciates her and he plans to show her later." She chuckled then, tilting her head again to the left. "Grandma says you have a tendency to say you're fine and then you wonder where everyone is and why no one is helping you. You are going to have to figure out how to accept help, young lady!"

I asked Nell what Mark thought about my new guy. She shook her head, "He won't talk about him because he's feeling territorial. Grandma, on the other hand, has lots to say. She said this is nice for you to explore. You feel sexy. But you're still not feeling confident. It's because you've allowed those other things that happened to you to be wounds and you keep picking them. With the current fellow, he's funny. He doesn't bite. There's something inno-cent about him. It's a nice change for you. You're not always sure about him, but he's what you need. He lets you be whoever you want to be, and he thinks you're beautiful."

Nell continued, "You've been so wounded and hurt. Even when you tried to separate from Mark, it wasn't over. You couldn't move on. He liked that you were under his thumb. He liked knowing you were pining for him. It's time to be done with that. You can honor that but be done with that. You can move on now, too. You wouldn't let yourself move on because of him. Are you going to let yourself? Or are you going to say, I can't...I'm grieving...woe is me?"

"So, I did the right thing, leaving when I did?" I asked, almost mystified by all the ways we were now picking my life apart, as if Nell had all the answers to my very own life review.

"You did the right thing. You had to use your discernment there. He was not a fit parent in many ways. You're going to honor your life and show your children how to live gloriously and without so much fear and cynicism."

Nell and I talked for another half an hour after that. I connected briefly with my mother, who seemed more distant and harder to reach. As if she wasn't in the room with me and Nell the way that Mark and my grandmother had been. Then I connected to my friend Sofia, who came straight through with her throaty voice and equal parts tender and gruff, just as she had been in life. The pieces of our story were put back together and I was able to say what I needed to her and hold her response, exactly as I had imagined it would be. I grieved deeply with her the loss of her life and our friendship. Nell concluded, "You have to forgive yourself. There are things you are in process with. This doesn't mean you don't realize your goodness too. Realize it and work from there. You are running a marathon. And you just want to lay down on the pavement and be done. But your loved ones will always be there to cheer you on from the other side. They are saying, Go, Jeanette, go! Go, Jeannie, go!"

Before ending, Nell suggested two books I should read about getting to know my shadow self. She told me I had to process both my grief from the passing of my loved ones, as well as the things I was grieving in myself. She concluded the session with another prayer and then asked if she could hug me. I stood up, with tears still streaming down my face.

"You're very loved," she said, softly. "I hope you could feel that today. Let us give thanks."

Nell walked me to the door where Erin was sitting on the porch, waiting for me. Erin took one look at me and knew I had found my answers. She burst out crying and Nell suggested we leave the car and go walk near the lake for a bit until I felt calm enough to drive back home. As we walked, Erin held my hand, and we cried while I recounted this surreal and amazing experience to her.

"Mark is there, E, and he is safe. And now I can talk to him whenever I need to."

We walked and walked and then Erin stopped suddenly, bending down to retrieve something shiny from the grass.

"This is crazy," she said, as she picked up an onyx and silver ring that was lying abandoned in the grass.

"That's his thank you gift for you," I said, listening to my own intuition and still feeling his presence filling me. Erin slipped the ring on and looped her arm back in mine. We walked back to the car and drove home, singing Mark's favorite songs all the way.

I spent the next few days and weeks in a bubble. Nell gave me a CD of our session and I listened to it over and over again. I wanted so badly for it to be real that I had to proof-test it to see if I could burst my own bubble. I searched for myself and my family members on Google. What could Nell have learned about me from my online presence? She might learn a little bit about my loved one's names and backgrounds. But there was no way she could detail the struggles I was having internally or pinpoint my children's needs in the way she did. Or tell me about Mark's darkness and emotional abuse without any prompting. She couldn't have known that the first time I went home with Brian that he said the words to me, "I promise, I don't bite." There was no way Nell could have known that Mark used to call me Jeannie simply because he knew I hated it when people used that nickname instead of Jen or Jenny. There was no way she could have possibly recounted, down to the finite details, the drama with my friend Sofia that led to our estrangement. The veil had been pulled back and now I couldn't unsee what I had experienced. For the first time since Mark's death, I felt at peace.

After that, I read everything I could get my hands on about spiritualism and evidence of life after death. No surprise, many of the books I read authored by the bereaved include similar experiences in receiving the blessing of proof of life after death. In *Seeking Jordan*, Matthew McKay tells of his son, Jordan's, murder and the ways in the aftermath that he tried and failed to put his own life back together as he attempted to make sense of such senseless violence. After a visit to a psychologist who specializes in EMDR (Eye Movement Desensitization and Reprocessing), McKay connects to the spirit of his son. From there, the book describes his experience seeking Jordan spiritually and the connection they create despite Jordan living in the afterlife. Through channeled writing, McKay shares with the world Jordan's telling of what the afterlife is like.[20]

I especially found Claire Bidwell Smith's *After This* helpful. Losing both of her parents in her young adult years and now as a mother of teens herself, Claire sets out to try to make sense of her parents' death through wondering where they

---

20 Matthew McKay, *Seeking Jordan: How I Learned the Truth About Death and the Invisible Universe*, (New World Press, 2016).

are now. The book chronicles her experiences with mediums, past life regressions, seances, meditation, and religious experiences. Ultimately, she concludes that "the afterlife is the relationship we continue to cultivate with our loved ones after they are gone. It is the way we internalize them, the ways in which we continue to bring them into the world, and the way we live in the world in their absence."[21] I also enjoyed Eben Alexander's *Proof of Heaven*, a book a friend had given me after my mother died, that I had cast aside at that time because I didn't believe in "bullshit." Alexander, a neurosurgeon, chronicles his near-death experience and his experience of the Holy while he was comatose.[22]

That first trip to Lily Dale was seven years ago now. It was nothing short of a miracle for me. I went in as a doubting Thomas and came out an hour later believing, without a single doubt, that God exists and that consciousness, the essence of who we are in our life, continues after our body dies. Not only that, but my loved ones are right there in it, and I now have an ability to communicate with them. Things changed after that. Mark's voice in my head got louder, as did my own. The intuition that Nell had implored me to listen to was running strong in my veins now. They were right. It was time for me to move my life forward. No more baby steps or toe-dipping. I didn't just want to live without him. I wanted passion, joy, hope, excitement, and wonder. I was tired of surviving.

---

21 Claire Bidwell Smith, *After This: When Life is Over, Where Do We Go?*, (Avery, 2015), 139-140.
22 Eben Alexander, *Proof of Heaven: A Neurosurgeon's Journey into the Afterlife*, (Simon & Schuster, 2012).

Lessons Learned:
Connecting to Your Loved One on the Other Side

Since my visit to Lily Dale, there are other ways in which I've bolstered my own spirit by connecting to my deceased loved ones. The tips below are things I've personally found helpful in maintaining a connection to them, whether as an internal sense of each of them in my own mind and heart or in feeling their external, spiritual presence in my day-to-day life.

1. **Set the intention.** Whether you are going to visit a medium, trying to dream of your lost loved one, or hoping to hear their voice in your head when you need guidance, pausing and taking the time to set your intention and slow your breath helps. This can be as simple as stopping, sitting, closing your eyes, and thinking of your loved one. Or you can call their name(s) out loud and let them know you are looking for them. Ask the universe to connect with them and tell them you need their guidance.

2. **Try praying.** Growing up in a Catholic family, I was told to pray a lot. We prayed every morning at school, and at every meal, and before bed. As a result, there were years where I went without praying. But as I've reconnected to my higher power and the universe within me, I've returned to more dedicated prayer. I still pray when things are going poorly, but I also give praise and thanks when things are going right. When I want or need to connect to my loved ones, I pray.

3. **Try reiki with a well-respected practitioner.** Reiki is a type of energetic healing based on the idea that the reiki therapist can channel energy into the patient's body to heal and restore both the body and emotional well-being. Nell had suggested that my health problems had a lot to do with energy blockages from my early life trauma and she thought reiki may help. It certainly did! Do your research and read reviews to find a good practitioner near you.

Reiki provided me with another tool in my toolbox to release the psychological pain I had been carrying in my body.

4. **Try a mediumship reading by a well-respected medium.** After sharing with many of my widowed friends about my experience with mediums, others have gone, too. Some had great success in feeling heard and connected to their loved ones; others, not so much. If you are interested in seeing a medium, read their reviews. Search out the best you can afford in your area. Be aware of what information is out there about you on the Internet or other media that could be known to anyone who is looking AND also trust that the universe is guiding you to be in the right place at the right time when you have the right intention. I do not recommend seeing a medium the first year post-loss and any reputable medium will tell you that you should not visit one more than every six to nine months for readings, if that. Take what is said with a grain of salt AND also allow yourself the hope that you will get the answers you seek when you are ready to receive them.

5. **Invite the Holy into your life.** I feel the Holy when I'm with friends around a campfire or when my niece grabs my face, kisses me, and I see my mother's eyes looking back at me. Wherever you find Holiness, hold it close. When we allow ourselves to put down the defenses of our daily lives and feel the true power of all the world around us, both visible and invisible, we can connect to our loved ones (and a higher power if you believe in one) in stronger ways.

6. **Journal your dreams.** Read up on lucid dreaming and see if you can channel a visitation dream with your deceased loved one. Keep a journal near your bedside and when you dream of your loved ones, write down the dreams. Meditate on the meaning of your dreams and ask your loved ones what they want you to know. Regularly speak to your loved ones and remind them you want them to visit you in your dreams. Some people also sleep with a favorite item of the deceased's or something with their handwriting

on it under their pillow. Try to reduce your stress, especially before bed and try to fall asleep with a happy memory of your times with your loved one.

7. **Spend time in nature.** Nature is a powerful healer. Studies have shown that time in nature can reset our autonomic nervous system and even walking by a greenspace can reduce our depression. At the height of my grief, I found my deepest solace gardening alone in the moonlight or listening to the mourning doves outside of my bedroom window. Their coos made me feel less alone. When the tulips I planted at the new house bloomed that first spring, fifteen months after Mark died, I was reminded that even in our darkest winter, when all seems dead and dormant, life is held in the seed and is ready to come forth again on its own timetable. Death may not be so finite or mysterious after all.

8. **Do good for others, in their memory.** Kindness is a powerful force. When you pair it with the intention of honoring your beloved, it can heal you. I have found that using Mark's life to help others after his death has provided me not only with the ability to let go of his things and keep his memory alive, but to honor who he was and how he lived when he was at his best. We continued his memorial birthday fundraiser for eight years. During that time, we raised over $20,000 for various charities he would have supported in his life. We donated ten guitars to an elementary school once. We helped fund a seizure-therapy dog. We gave a scholarship to a chiropractic student who was a young, working parent. When we give, whether of our time, spirit, or money, and live in ways that honor our loved ones, we keep them alive inside of us and their love extends outward.

9. **Seek wonder.** You'll find them there.

PART IV

Charting A New Course

ELEVEN

Making Peace with the Loss of My Marriage

M y widowed friend, Annmarie, got it. In one of our discussions about how sucky being a widowed parent was, she told me something I've come back to again and again. She said, "You don't ever really accept that it's happened (the death of your spouse), but you accept that you can't change it. That life is still going. The clock is still ticking. The sun still rises. And the sun still sets. And there is still a life that has to be lived."

After Lily Dale, I rode the waves of moving my life forward with this deeper intention that I still had a life to be lived. I settled into the new house and really made it my own. My garden exploded with growth, as if reflecting the energy I felt inside, even if my body was still slow in recovering. I gave up gluten and, for a while, I gave up dairy. I was playing piano. I was painting. I was very much enjoying my now public relationship with Brian. I made arm's-length friends with some of the neighboring women, and I regularly saw my old friends. The kids and I took a trip with Erin and stayed for a weekend in a yurt on the beautiful, organic farm of another single mother. We went swimming in a state park under a waterfall. I decided to confront my fear of death that day by jumping off the waterfall and plunging into the deep. I screamed all the way down the thirty or so feet and when I plunged under, my feet instinctively started searching for the bottom. But it wasn't there. For a moment, I panicked. And then I saw the light. I swam up and up and up until I surfaced, gasping for breath.

With the exception of giving birth, I've never felt so alive as I did at that moment, which isn't to say I didn't get psychologically tossed back into the waters of grieving hard and deep on a regular basis after that. In a way, that time was not all that different from the first year, post-loss of Mark, in that I was beginning again and then not. And then beginning again. The difference was that this time, the stretches in-between grew longer. It might have even seemed to some that I was thriving here on this little island for shipwreck survivors I had created.

But the waves could be insidious. Post-traumatic stress disorder (PTSD) usually is. In the previous chapter, I wrote a lot about the body, a little bit about the mind, and a lot about the spiritual seeking I did after Mark died. PTSD had been riding along on my waves for many years before that catastrophic period in my thirties when so many of my loved ones died. It has been my mental and emotional companion since childhood. There were years in my life, especially in my twenties, when I thought I had bested it. But when these losses occurred to my adult self, it was my child self who was still nursing wounds from earlier abuse in my family of origin. She got really, really triggered, usually in the context of my deepening relationship with Brian.

The first year Brian and I were dating, we were immersed in our own grief for our spouses, in the bond we had formed through this grief, and in the highs and accompanying fears of *What does this relationship mean?* Still, I fell hard for him. After the kids knew about our relationship, we started seeing each other several times a week. We'd usually go out on a date on the weekend, as well. We had even managed to go away overnight together twice. When we exchanged our first "I Love You's" we both admitted we felt guilty being so happy.

During our second into third year together, I began to seek answers outside of myself and asked the big, big questions of *Where are they now?* and *What's the point of my life?* It seemed that the more I expanded, the more Brian retreated into himself, coming out only to be with me. This change in him made me pull back again. I waited for him to disappoint me, just like I had been disappointed so many times during my relationship with Mark. It took twenty-five months, but Brian finally succeeded.

When the disappointment came, though, I realized that underlying the disappointment was really my own fear of abandonment. Apparently, I believed Brian should be infallible even as I kept giving myself grace. On more than one occasion, I convinced myself that I felt more for Brian than he did for me. I always tried to respect his loss because I understood what such a loss felt like even if I didn't know what *his* loss felt like. There were pieces of our losses that we shared with each other but there were pieces he was processing by himself, and when he retreated into that, I experienced his need for privacy as pushing me away. I compared his love for me to his love for his late wife, Leah, all the time. And I knew I was also waiting for him to do all the things that Mark had done in my marriage to displease me. I was very conscious that I was bringing my own meat and sides onto this plate o' grief we shared. We were two people in a relationship for a party of four. Check, please!

Brian knew I was struggling with my fear that he would abandon me and some of his behaviors only exacerbated these fears. I was relieved then when he spoke my love language: he asked me to attend a therapy session with him. He wanted to make amends for his behaviors that hurt me. When we met with his counselor, Greg, the following week, Greg began the session by acknowledging that we were a young-enough couple with a fairly unusual story. That each of us was carrying great grief into a new relationship was uncommon and this made our relationship more difficult than most, right from the start. As my doubts poured out during the session, Greg gently but firmly confronted me on my expectations for how Brian's grief path should mirror my own.

Greg also pointed out how different our marriages had been. Mark and I had been together twenty-one years, three-and-a-half times longer than Brian and Leah had together. Mark and I had been married twelve years to their near three. Brian and Leah hadn't been together long enough on their marriage trajectory to hit the turbulent waves that so many long-term couples experience. He missed his newlywed wife, and his secondary losses included a future with Leah and building a home and a family with her. Greg then asked me if I had explicitly worked on my grief related to losing the chance to repair my marriage to Mark, since we had seemingly been moving in that direction when he died. I told Greg that so much of my therapy had focused on Mark's actual death and the daily stresses I had since then that I hadn't actually done a lot on the relationship itself. Greg reflected how Brian and I were each carrying an enormous amount of guilt about our late spouses having died alone. On top of that, this was Brian's first time in therapy, and he was not used to talking about his feelings. I was a twenty-year veteran of the therapy trenches. Yet here we were, holding hands on the therapy couch, talking hard truths to each other, crying all the way through it, and being committed to doing the work.

"So, what's the verdict? Do you think we need to come back from more sessions?" I asked Greg.

He surprised me by saying, "I think you two have one of the healthiest relationships I've ever seen. Sure, you are both learning how to communicate with each other, but this is tough, tough stuff. And you are here, supporting each other in speaking your truth."

Buddhist nun and teacher, Pema Chodron, writes in *The Places That Scare You*, that to be brave is to be without self-deception. This, however, she says is not so easy to do.

A warrior begins to take responsibility for the direction of her life. It's as if we are lugging around unnecessary baggage....Open the bags and look closely at what we are carrying. In doing this, we begin to understand that much of it isn't needed anymore.[23]

I had been consistently going to my own therapy, twice a month, for almost four years with Alice. Alice had helped me cope with my mother's death, with Mark's diagnosis of epilepsy and our separation and then with Mark's death. At this point in therapy, we had been focusing a lot on managing my stress to help with my health issues and I was afraid to reopen the wound from the separation. Brian's therapist was right. I needed to start practicing what I preached and do the work, even though there was a large part of me that didn't want to "go there."

During my visit to Lily Dale, Nell had confronted me on the way my marriage was unhealthy and specifically on the ways that Mark emotionally abused me. While Alice and I talked at length in previous sessions about Mark's

---

23 Chodron, *The Places That Scare You*, 17.

mental health and how his regular suicidality impacted me, she had never gone so far as to push me to call it abusive. One of the reasons I really wanted the relationship with Brian to work was that Brian never, not once, ever, made me afraid of him. I couldn't say this about Mark. Looking back, I don't think I ever told Alice much about the ways in which Mark regularly yelled at me when he couldn't control his moods; the ways in which he could explode in anger and, for example, punch a hole in the wall next to my head, or throw things or break things in front of me. My husband had so much anger and no one to hold it. He was an adult having a child's tantrum and the epilepsy made it easier after his death to excuse it. How much of Mark's behavior was Mark responsible for? And did that even matter now, other than how those behaviors impacted me and my children?

Alice and I spent the next few months talking more deeply about the impact of Mark's behaviors on my mental health. I was able to acknowledge it was emotionally abusive. We talked about the ways it triggered my anxieties from childhood and the ways in which I wanted both protection from and to protect Mark. We examined how I was pulling these old patterns into my relationship with Brian leading to my difficulty in trusting in a future with him and under-scoring my belief that a life with me would not be enough for him. We further explored how I could trust any man with my children.

During this time, I purchased and quickly read both of the self-help books that the medium, Nell, had recommended to me. Debbie Ford's *The Dark Side of the Light Chasers* focuses on how we heal ourselves so that we don't leave holes in our partners or our children. This is done, she says, by bringing awareness to our open wounds or light to our hidden darkness. Building on the work of psychoanalyst Carl Jung, Ford says that it is in facing the hidden parts of ourselves, those we typically deem our worst traits or as Jung described it, "the person you would rather not be" that we become whole and when we are whole, we are healed.[24]

I took inventory of my shadow self. There were many parts of me that I felt shame about or didn't like. Ford wrote that being whole was better than being

---

24 Debbie Ford, *The Dark Side of the Light Chasers: Reclaiming Your Power, Creativity, Brilliance, and Dreams*, (Riverhead Books, 2010), 5, 83.

good. "You must be prepared to love all that you have feared."[25] I didn't like my shadow self very much and I realized that not liking it didn't stop me from letting some of those parts make decisions for me, like the time I decided to break up with Brian early on in our relationship out of fear that he would want a child I couldn't (or didn't want to) produce. Talking about these pieces of myself with Alice, especially as they showed up in my relationships with Mark and Brian, led me to another important breakthrough in therapy.

Alice confronted me: "You are the third leg of this stool, Jeanette. There's Mark. There's Brian. And there's you. And you always act as if you don't matter. Or as if you can't hold the weight yourself. As if you'd fall apart without them."

Sure, I had learned to trust myself a little more since Mark died. I had learned to live alone during our separation and then again after he died. I was finding creative outlets and trying new things. But did I trust myself? Did I know, like really know in my bones, that I would be okay alone? Could I be my own friend? Debbie Ford noted that when one befriends themselves, they break the continuing cycle of loss of self or loss of others.

In her book, *The Spiritual Divorce*, written four years after the first edition of *The Dark Side* book, Ford examines her relationship with the transformative pain of divorce. In the first book, she looks at the shadow self to identify what is missing in you that will make you whole. In this second book, she looks at what is missing in a relationship that will make you whole and how you can find those missing pieces within yourself. Ford writes, "Pain and change are the keys that open the door to a deeper understanding of our human experience. The pain of divorce breaks down our defenses, leaving us in a place of complete vulnerability."[26] Nell didn't say much about why this book was what I needed when she recommended it to me, but as I read it, it became clearer there were ways to get closure to my marriage as well as to other relationship hurts I was still carrying from that time in my life. I had ghosts I needed to divorce, and Ford was clear that honesty was the only way to step out of pain and suffering. This book was written like a workbook and I ate it all up. What made me feel

---

25 Ibid, 117.
26 Debbie Ford, *Spiritual Divorce: Divorce as a Catalyst for an Extraordinary Life* (Harper Books, 2006), 5.

vulnerable in my relationship with Mark? What anger did I hold onto? I let out my rage, my resentment, my disappointments, my hurt, fears, and sadness in the pages of that journal. Most importantly, *The Spiritual Divorce* asks a key question: What attracted you to your partner and how do those qualities or characteristics show up in your own life? Or said another way: What were the gifts in my marriage or relationship that my partner brought to it and how would I receive those gifts now that he was gone?

It was easy for me to list all the *wrongs* Mark and I had both committed in the twenty-one years of our relationship. It was harder to list the *rights*, those things we did well to and for each other. Then, one day, I realized all I had to do was look at what he left behind that was most important to me. These were the rights in our relationship: poetry, music, art, deep listening, a clear knowledge of who I was and my gifts to the world. Mark brought beauty into my life by introducing me to new music, finding art in spoken and written word, and encouraging me to write, even when I felt he was the stronger writer. When he was healthy, he listened to me deeply. He knew me inside and out. He wanted good things for me. He believed I deserve good things, so much so that he didn't believe I deserved him.

I took a long, hard look at myself and my marriage as I moved into year three without Mark. I realized that I liked this Jeanette who no longer hid the truth about Mark's depression or epilepsy, including how hard it was on me. I liked this Jeanette who had boundaries. Who could say to her relatives, "I'm sorry, I can't right now" and not owe further explanation. And even though it was incredibly uncomfortable for me, I liked the letting go of not knowing how this story with Brian would turn out. Doing this work meant no "fast-forwarding" of my relationship with Brian. No fantasy homemaking. No fantasy wedding. No fantasy baby. Things needed to unfold between us at the pace they needed because we each had work to do to heal and, I reminded myself, there were two little kids whose lives and hearts were also on the line, depending on how much I brought this man into their daily lives. Nothing made me feel as vulnerable to loss as falling in love again.

Then, in late 2017, I was handed an opportunity to practice what I was preaching. One of the parents in my Widowed Parent Project shared that there was a conference for widowed folks coming up just three hours away from me. The conference (which was founded by a widow looking for her people) sounded like it might just do me some good. In part because I didn't want to pay the fee and hotel, and, in part, because I was starting to believe that I was actually learning things about myself that might benefit other people. I decided to sign up to be a presenter. Instead of ignoring the part of me that felt like an imposter attending the conference, I trusted Debbi Ford's advice and decided to bring that part of me to light. My presentation, entitled *Standing In Your Story*, was approved, so off to the conference I went.

I checked in late on the first afternoon of the conference, as my presentation wasn't until the second day. When I rolled up to the registration desk, one of the organizers said, "Oh good, you're here!" (as if she knew who I was) and promptly told me that they were excited for my session which I had billed as a workshop on authentically healing yourself after loss when your marriage was less than perfect, or some such thing.

"You'd be surprised how many people feel like imposters here. Everyone wants to put their dead spouses up on pedestals but there are a lot of us who had less than ideal marriages. Some of us were even happy when they kicked it! So, we are doing this new thing this afternoon where we are offering small groups to welcome people and help them kinda find their place here. We saw on your resume that you were a therapist-type and figured you could probably facilitate a session on people who were coming here with the less-than-ideal marriage."

"Um, ok," was all I replied at first. Then, as it settled in on me that I was now going to have to not just stand up behind the protection of a podium tomorrow, but live what I was talking about on the spot with a group of strangers, I gulped. I stared at her blankly. This woman was a pro. Ignoring my extended silence, she reached around and picked up my bag.

"Great, so we'll just check your luggage and get you right to your room. Just put the chairs in a circle and people should stagger in after the next break. It's ninety minutes. I'm sure you'll figure out how to fill it."

This is what I get, I thought to myself. Authenticity matters. Leading with vulnerability. Standing in your story. These were themes I was planning on touching on during my presentation, but I sure as hell was not ready to live them at that moment, with no preparation. I walked into Ballroom C and closed the doors behind me.

"Breathe and push," I told myself, a favorite affirmation from one of my favorite activists.[27] As people came in and the circle of chairs started filling out, I began by making small talk until the room of strangers was looking at me. This must be what it feels like to join an AA meeting for the first time. So, I tried to open with a "Hi, I'm Jeanette and I had a difficult marriage to my dead spouse." The room was silent. People were staring at me.

I continued, "And, as you can see on this lanyard tag I'm wearing, this is my first time here. Just got in twenty minutes ago, actually, and was informed I was leading this session. So, let's talk and figure this out together." I told people a little bit about me and Mark and that we were separated when he died. I told them I was nervous about coming to this conference and that I felt like an imposter. And then the universe gave me just what I needed that afternoon when I let myself be vulnerable. One person after another started to share how they, too, worried that they didn't belong at the conference. Ninety minutes flew by with people sharing their stories and me reflecting what I heard of their fears, their strengths, their struggles, and their triumphs. When I showed up to give my presentation the next day, I was shocked that the seats were filled.

I had debated until I got up to the podium just how authentic I would be about the struggles in my marriage. The truth and nothing but the truth. It was getting easier and easier to talk about Mark's struggles and how his mental and physical health impacted me. But the whole truth? I had yet to publicly share the ways my behavior contributed to the harm that was done to my marriage. I rose to the challenge and decided to share all of our story.

That night, when I got back to my room, there was a reminder from someone that I used to know waiting for me in my Twitter feed. The synchronicity of the universe again brought me to the moment when I could look at it, feel all the feelings, look at how far I had come, and then let it go. This person from my past had hurt me deeply in the before and aftermath of Mark's death and it

---

27 Valerie Kaur, *Watch Night Speech: Breathe and Push.* URL: https://valariekaur. com/2017/01/watch-night-speech-breathe-push/

was the kind of thing that, in the past, could have sent me and all my insecurities spiraling. Except it didn't. I called Brian to tell him about my day and checked in with the kids. And then I went to bed.

My first widowed conference experience held a mirror to me. I was able to see that I had filled in the broken places with gold. I was shining all on my own and I only had to embrace all of me to heal. My marriage was healing because I also had embraced all of Mark: the good, the bad, and the ugly. We were not perfect people. We did not have the perfect marriage. His death was about as far from a good death as anyone could wish. My heart had broken, over and over, in both our life together and in his death. I had blamed myself for the shipwreck. But by surrendering to the pain and holding it in my hands, by letting myself be vulnerable and imperfect, I had come to realize that just because our love was imperfect, did not mean our love wasn't also worthy. Life is imperfect. Death is imperfect, too. The beauty of it all was there beside the agony. Standing in your story frees you from it.

Lessons Learned:
Healing Your Marriage by Yourself (or With Your Therapist)

Even if you had a damn good marriage or partnership with your person, you probably have regrets and some hurts that remain unresolved. Things you said or didn't get to say. Things you needed to hear that were never expressed. Every widow/er I've met has carried guilt about what they did or didn't do at the end of their spouse's life. For those of us who had years of struggles with our spouse, it may only be after their death that we give ourselves permission to deal with ALL of it. It's okay to be messy with your healing but do the work to heal. Your future self and your next relationship will thank you.

1. **Tell the story of your marriage.** Make a playlist, write the time-line, or put together a photo essay. Even if you show no one else, it's important to put together the narrative (the good and the bad) of your time with your beloved. Seeing the whole story again helps to put the loss as well as any related difficulties into the context of the whole.

2. **Take a relationship inventory of your marriage**. List all of the things that still bring you pain when you think about them. What needs to heal? Ask yourself what emotions accompany each item on your list. Note where you feel resentment, abandonment, shame, guilt, anger. If your person was still here, what actions would you want them to take to give your story a better ending? What actions do you need to take? You don't need to do anything with this list right away. Just sit with it for a while.

3. **Write an angry letter to your spouse**. Somewhere deep down, most of us, even if we had a great marriage, are angry at our spouse for dying and leaving us behind, whether through no fault of their own or even if at their own hand. Either way, we must feel our anger and then release those emotions so it doesn't eat us up. Go back and look at your inventory. For the unhealed hurts that left you angry, write a letter to your loved one that you mail to

nowhere, bury next to them, burn later, or just revisit as you need
to allow you to express your rage, your resentment, your disappointments, your hurt, your fears, and your sadness. If writing a
letter doesn't feel right, try journaling or creating art to express
these feelings.

4. **Go back to your list, again. Identify ways you can take action
on your own to resolve as many of the issues as you can on the
list.** Some may be simpler than others. Do you need to go to the
grave and say to yourself what you wish your spouse could say?
Do you need to take action to bolster your own life in some ways?
For example, if your spouse regularly self-harmed, what can you
do to help heal this hurting part of you? Can you make more time
for self-care? Or maybe you need to be accountable for actions
you took that harmed your spouse. A lot of people are unfaithful
in their marriages. If you were unfaithful and your infidelity was
unknown, find a therapist to help you process what was happening
in your marriage at that time and own your role in what happened.
If you are carrying shame and guilt about this, process it. Own it
and then ask yourself if it is serving you to still hold onto these
emotions now.

5. **Forgive yourself.** Over and over, forgive yourself. Whatever you
have to heal, know that this step may take a lot of time. It's taken
me years to really work through what was not healed in my marriage, especially because I carried so much shame and guilt about
our separation and the way Mark died.

6. **When you know better, do better**. You have an opportunity to
change the way you engage in a relationship now—whether that's
a relationship with a new partner, with your friends, children, or
even yourself. Look at the things in your inventory that you have
healed and ask yourself how to not repeat these mistakes in the
future. What values or skills do you want in your life now? Do you
need better boundaries? More honesty? Have you been ingenuine?
Work on yourself and you will heal. Not only you in the present

and future, but you'll heal past hurts as well. You'll be able to give yourself more grace for your actions in your marriage.

7. **Inventory the gifts of your marriage.** Now identify what in your life feels incomplete without your spouse. Sometimes these are our secondary losses. For example, since Mark died, I had no one in my life to introduce me to all the best, coolest, up and coming music. No one wrote me poetry anymore. I didn't have anyone with deep knowledge of who I was and my history. I worried about who would help me hold my anxiety. These were all the gifts Mark gave me. And everything he gave was important to me and I didn't want to lose all of it, just because I had lost him. Find new ways to meet these needs in yourself. Use your loss to birth a new way of living.

8. **Seek professional help.** A skilled therapist can help you resolve remaining marital issues, such as issues that feel too big or issues that snowball and trigger other issues in your life, like, I don't know, say from your childhood? No one said you had to do this alone. Yes, therapy is expensive. But so is living with ghosts and passing that trauma onto your children. Or carrying unexpressed emotions around until they result in a heart attack or stroke. Let someone do the work beside you and steer the ship together.

TWELVE

Building a Life to Love

Just as I really found my footing and our island was no longer feeling like an island, another storm was brewing. A few months after the widowed conference, early in the new year of 2018, I learned that the college that had been my employer for the last fifteen years was going to shut down the department where I worked. I was to be out of a job by the end of the year. I was also turning 40. As if Mark's death and the other losses that preceded it hadn't aged me enough, the thought of having to find a new job after fifteen years did me in. It felt like the tide had come in again, threatening to wreck my newfound peace.

Like many widows whose spouses leave them without retirement or life insurance to float on for a while, I made just enough money to get us by. At the end of any given week, I had about $80 in my name and only $500 in emergency savings. I couldn't bear the thought of downsizing further and having to move the kids again. Brian had assured me he would help us if it took me time to find a new job and I could access unemployment for the year that followed, if needed. Brian reminded me he also had a new house with four bedrooms and two baths, but it was back in the school district we had formerly been living in. I told him I appreciated his offer to help me sell the house and move in with him full time, but I wasn't quite there yet. I didn't say no, though, because if the choice came down to either living with my father or living with Brian for a time, I'd pick Brian. And then Brian went into work one Friday morning and by the end of the day, found out he too was losing his job and much sooner than I was.

It was time for me to decide where this relationship was going. We had been dating for three years and had settled into the comfortable routine of weekends at his place and him staying with us one or two weeknights. The children had accepted Brian in their lives but they weren't especially bonded to him. We didn't see each other every day though, so there was just enough space in the relationship for me to feel committed, but also the freedom to leave any time I needed to without a lot of untangling. Now, Brian and I were both facing unemployment. Even so, he was in a much better financial position than I was, thanks to having a life with more privilege that did not leave him with a pile of student loans and no childcare costs to tack onto his budget.

After overanalyzing the situation for a few days, I diligently began searching for a new job. We would stay in the area, and I'd just have to find a new job to make it all work out financially. I was determined to disrupt the children's lives as little as possible, even though mine felt like it was turning upside down again. I did a few interviews with hopes of netting a remote job so I could avoid child-care costs for before/after school programming and be home when the kids needed to be picked up every day. That got me nowhere. Then one night, deep into a pitcher of margaritas to drown my anxiety, there on page nine of an Indeed search, I saw a posting for the Executive Director of Grassroots Gardens of Western New York. The very same local community gardening organization that the kids and I had spent that one Saturday with as volunteers at the Food Bank community garden just two years earlier. Looking back, that day had been a turning point for me. Until then, the kids and I hadn't ever walked into a group of unknown people before and offered our time in service. As we worked alongside the other volunteers (the University's football team, a few Master Gardeners, a family of refugees who had benefited from the Food Bank's services when they were first resettled and wanted to pay their time forward), I began to feel safe again in my body. It was as if I had been on high alert since Mark had died but there in the garden, meeting new people and reconstructing raised beds for the pantry's produce, I felt a wholeness spread in me that gave me hope that our life, too, could get to a point where someday we could pay it forward.

While it would be a huge pay cut from what my job at the college paid, I imagined myself spending my days out in the sun, gardening with other social justice warriors. My heart leapt a little. I had zero professional experience in urban agriculture, which was on their list of preferred qualifications, but I did have most of the nonprofit management skills they needed. I also had a deep knowledge of gardening and community development. Could I take a risk like this to do something I was sure I would love and leave behind the comfort of the career I knew?

I recalled how I felt the year before when I jumped off the waterfall. Refreshed. I wanted to be refreshed. Sometimes you just have to dive in and trust you will surface. I wrote a very authentic cover letter that violated all of the rules of professional decorum, and in just a few paragraphs, I told them why I believed gardens healed and why I thought I had the skills to be their next director, despite not having worked in the food justice movement before. Three months and six interviews later, I had the job. I would start right before my birthday.

In my twenties, I had thought of forty as old. I had expected that, by forty, I would surely be a tenured professor at Yale or Princeton. Mark would have magically grown up and been all I needed him to be as a partner and co-parent. But life never works out the way we imagine. After the hell I went through in my thirties, I was no longer afraid of turning forty. In fact, I welcomed it. It was a new decade. It was the first decade I'd have without Mark alongside me, but here I was, still standing.

Relationships that you start as an adult are different than when you are immersed in one that requires you to grow up with your partner. Brian and I were still learning new things about each other all of the time and instead of fearing that those things would break us down, I began to enjoy finding out about the various ways he ticked. Over those three months I was interviewing, we determined that it was time to cast our lot together. I was honest with the kids about the unknowns we were facing and told them that I wanted Brian to move in with us or us with him. They surprisingly accepted it pretty quickly, which was a relief, but also asked where we would put him. Brian and I recognized that moving in together would require at least one of us to make some pretty significant sacrifices to how we were living. I couldn't see myself living in the house Brian and Leah had designed (and forcing the kids to move schools again) and there was no room for him and his house full of things to be comfortable in our little village house.

There was also the issue of his cats, which were his world after Leah died. Grace was severely allergic to them and there was no way he could live with us and keep the cats. With the offer of the job at Grassroots Gardens, I knew I would need to allow myself to depend on Brian financially to help support our daily living expenses. It was hard for me to allow a man to help "take care" of me again. I had been on my own now with the kids for over four years since my separation from Mark and I was scared to ever put myself in a position to depend on another person. On the other hand, how would living together go if I wasn't going to trust Brian as a co-parent and partner, including figuring out how we would financially mingle our lives? He agreed with me that the most important thing was to keep the kids in their current school district, but that meant he would have to give up the cats and seventy-five percent of his possessions to fit in our house, or we'd have to move again. After weighing all our options, we decided we would have to start over, once again.

After a perilous search, Brian and I bought a big, old "mid century colonial" in a cul-de-sac in the middle of farmland. It had been pretty neglected and would need some renovation, but we were project people. It was in the neighboring rural town next to the village where I lived and one of the last houses registered still in my kids' current school district. To my surprise, when I half-jokingly asked my father if he wanted to move in with us since it had six bedrooms, he agreed.

Even though there was so much unsettled during these months, I didn't want to let my fortieth birthday go by uncelebrated. I went back to the bucket list I had created during the November storm, in the aftermath of Mark's death. *Travel more* was one of the things I had written. We didn't have the money for air travel, but we could still get away somewhere new and beautiful to celebrate my making it forty years. As I considered our options, I settled on a trip up the coast of New England to Acadia National Park. The morning we set out on our trip, Brian stopped to turn over the keys to his house to our realtor. His house had sold quickly, and he had piled all of his stuff between my basement and a storage unit. After the trip, he would temporarily move in with us.

This next step in our story was happening and instead of being over-whelmed with anxiety, I told myself I knew how to handle change now. On the long drive to Maine, we stopped for an overnight at a stable with an inn in New Hampshire, so we could spend the morning of my birthday horseback riding in the foothills of the White Mountains. It was magical. When we made it to the ocean in Acadia the next day, I ran to the shore. As I looked back at Brian and the kids, searching for the elusive blue starfish of Wonderland Beach, I whispered to the waves, "I made it, Mark. We're all going to be okay."

Three weeks later, I was standing with my feet planted firmly on the ground, next to Gerldine, one of Grassroot Gardens' longtime community gardeners, in the garden she had started about five years earlier. I spent a lot of my first weeks at my new job touring the 80+ community gardens in our network, but Gerldine's garden and story stood out. Gerldine credited the garden with help-ing her heal from the sudden, violent death of her brother.

"This is sacred land," she said quietly, and I nodded in understanding. We walked back to her house and she invited me in, showing me picture after picture of what the garden had looked like when it was an overgrown lot full of weeds and debris. There had once been a house on the lot, empty and overrun with rodents, before Gerldine, her nonstop spirit, and her block club finally convinced the city to tear it down. After the bulldozers left, the city never came back to care for the lot. It took several more years of community advocacy before the block club got the green light to turn the lot into a community garden. The once-vacant, rodent-infested lot had been transformed through sweat and tears into a lush garden with over a dozen raised beds brimming with kale, tomatoes, peas, beans, collards and more. A beautiful patch of bright red poppies adorned the entrance to the garden while a tall pine provided shade at the back.

Gerldine told me about how the garden was the only place she could go to be alone with her grief. How necessary transforming the lot was to transform her anger and her pain. Even though we had just met, I told Gerldine how my garden helped save me and my mental health after Mark died. She asked me how my children were, and I told her about the support we had received from our community grief center.

She replied with a sharp tongue, "No one is coming here to offer our community that kind of support." I listened then, as she told me the story about a young woman on the block who had lost her mother. Gerldine took the young woman into the garden and gave her wildflower seeds. They planted them together so the young woman, whose family could not afford a head-stone or place in a cemetery for remembrance of her mother, would have a place to go to pray to her mother, to talk with her, and to remember her each year as the flowers came up. Gerldine assured her that her mother's legacy would live on in her.

One of the things I most appreciated about Grassroots Gardens was that it was a community-led organization, meaning the community was centered in all organizational decisions. I quietly put my idea for a therapeutic gardening program on the back burner as other agency needs required my attention. But as I met more community gardeners from across the two cities of Buffalo and Niagara Falls that first season and heard their stories of what their gardens did for their mental health, for their physical health, and for their spirits, I knew therapeutic gardening was already happening at Grassroots Gardens, even though there was no formal program built around it. The organization was strapped for cash, so my first call was to the University at Buffalo to see if I could get a graduate student in social work placed with our agency. I was thrilled when they found a student who was an excellent match for the program I wanted to create. I then called on Emily. Emily is a grief counselor and creative arts ther-apist who runs a local community grief support group and related program-ming. She was the one who led the family support group the children and I had attended. I wanted to bring Emily, Gerldine, our new graduate student, Nicole, and other community gardeners and mental health partners together to talk about how we could use the land we were gardening on to also be spaces for nourishing psychological well-being and recovery. The Grassroots Gardens Therapeutic Gardening Task Force was sown that summer of 2019.

By 2019, I had survived almost five years without Mark in my life. During that first year at Grassroots Gardens, while I was literally and figuratively sowing seeds in my community, I felt my life moving forward and the intensity of the grief I held all these last years started to fade. Brian and I were rebuilding a beautiful life together in our new home and, for all purposes, we had settled well into it.

Six months after moving in together, and both reemployed, we started talking more seriously about marriage. Despite my fears, another move hadn't disrupted the children's lives too much. They enjoyed having my dad living with us and everyone got along well with Brian. I started dropping hints to Brian about how he'd have to get me a wedding bracelet or necklace since I couldn't wear rings anymore. One day, while we were out and about in the village, we walked past a custom jewelry store.

"Why don't we see if there isn't some way around the arthritis? Maybe they can make you a custom engagement ring?" he said. He kissed my ringless hand and that was all I needed to hear. It turned out jewelers can make specialty rings for people with arthritis. We set up an appointment the following week to come back and look at rings and, of course, I slid into the excitement of it all. Before the chosen ring was even fully paid for or an official proposal made, we decided where we would marry the following summer. We settled into a lovely period of rebirth after our engagement—enjoying our new jobs, enjoying our new home, and enjoying the ways the children were growing. At first, I told myself I was too old for all the traditions of a bride but as the year went on, I relaxed and gave myself permission to enjoy wedding planning with him. We were reveling in it all.

I left my ring at home so I could dig in the mud with Gerldine, Emily, and others when we held the first *They That Sow in Tears* workshop later that summer of 2019. The free workshop provided time and space for people who are grieving to learn with us about the ways gardening can be an adaptive tool for coping with grief. Gerldine, who is a writer and poet, led us through journaling activities and reflections throughout our time together, helping participants find the words to express their loss. Emily led us through memorial-making as we played in the mess of concrete and plaster, making stepping stones to remember our loved ones. As participants planted a hydrangea as a collective memorial in the garden, I shared the ways that gardening can act as meditation and metaphor for our grief, inviting them to reflect on how the garden allows us to both create and destroy in a safe space; how when no one else will listen, the earth can hold our tears, our anger, and even our hope; how even in the darkest, coldest night, when we feel dead inside, the universe knows we are like seeds just waiting for the sun to beckon them to the surface where they will live again.

In the book *Broken Open*, author Elizabeth Lesser shares that "if we can stay awake when our lives are changing, secrets will be revealed to us—secrets about ourselves, about the nature of life, and about the eternal source of happiness and peace that is always available, always renewable, always within us."[28] What if the loss of your spouse catalyzes the restart of your life? What if you are planting the seeds now for the future self you will blossom into? Taking the leadership job at Grassroots Gardens helped me grow in all kinds of ways. I learned to lean into grief alongside the community. I learned that I was fully capable of holding multiple anxieties and pressures on any given day; of making big decisions that impacted others with confidence and an assuredness I was missing in myself before. I learned that whether one digs in the soil to find solace or finds themselves floating in a sea while life passes by, each of us can do the work to free ourselves from pain. Leaning into your grief, your fears, your anxieties, and depression will not break you, even when it feels like it will. We get to a point with our grief where we have to decide whether we want our children to see us as a parent who was forever damaged by our loss or whether we want to be a parent who models for our children how you pick up the pieces and move forward. This does not come easily. You must do the work of grieving first. I always end the *They That Sow in Tears* workshops by revealing the full scripture the phrase is based on. Psalm 126:5 reads "Those that sow in tears will reap with songs of joy."[29] Let your tears plant joy.

---

28 Elizabeth Lesser, *Broken Open: How Difficult Times Can Help Us Grow*, (New York: Villard), xxiii.
29 Psalm 126: 5-6 (New International Version).

Lessons Learned:
From Surviving to Thriving

Building a life you love can feel both exciting and daunting. As you learn to get comfortable with the new you after your loss, you may find there are other ways of living you want to explore. We can also make all the external changes we want to our life and still feel empty. For me, moving from surviving to thriving was first an internal process. See if any of this resonates with you as you set out to create a life you love.

1. **Lean into authenticity**. It is easier (and often necessary) in our grief and life after loss to want to shield ourselves and our children from pain and prying eyes. As such, we may put on a mask and drop the proverbial "I'm fine," when people ask us how we are doing. Be honest about how you are, who you are, and what you need.

2. **Stop settling**. Are there relationships in your life that are draining you? Does your job suck the life out of you? Use this time of reimagining your life to think big and stop settling. Prioritize what makes you and your kids happy and healthy. Everything else can change. As the poet Mary Oliver asks, "What do you want to do with your one wild and precious life?"[30]

3. **Boundary up.** Part of being authentic and not settling for less than you deserve is learning how to have stricter boundaries. Many of us did not learn this skill as children and we have been remiss in also teaching our children how to have boundaries. Boundaries can feel uncomfortable at first but once you learn to speak up for yourself, your family, and your needs, it gets easier. Look at the places in your life where you feel taken advantage of. This is usually a place where you need a boundary. Try it and see how it feels.

---

30 Oliver, Mary. "The Summer Day." *New and Selected Poems.* Boston: Beacon Press, 1992.

4. **Replace control with grace.** For me, part of learning to thrive instead of surviving had a lot to do with letting go of control. Yes, you shouldn't settle and you need boundaries. But when we try to manipulate all of the things, all of the time, we remove space for wonder to come into our lives. When we control people, we leave no room for grace.

5. **Let go of the shame.** As you change, people will have all kinds of opinions about it. It can be easy to get sucked into the shame and guilt cycle again. I found it helpful to remind myself that people hadn't been through what I had been through, and as such, they can't understand. Therefore, their opinion is not of value to me. Let. It. Go.

6. **Embrace creativity.** Think back to your childhood. When you had no responsibilities, what brought you joy? Sports? Time in nature? Making art? Free play? Try to choose one area of creativity that you want to invest your time in. Take a cooking class. Buy the model kit. Sign up for a weekend writing retreat. It is never too late to find a new passion and embrace your creative side. Creativity unleashes our potential and it allows us to play again. Play restores our spirit.

7. **Seek joy.** Think back on the experiences that have been most joyful in your life before loss. Think ahead to all the things you'd like to try before you die. Now you know what brings you joy (or has the potential to). Try to commit to creating a few of those experiences for yourself this year and in the years to come. If love brought you joy, maybe it's time to step back into the dating pool. If helping others brings you joy, maybe it's time to leave your corporate job and go back to school for a social work degree. Perhaps you still want another child. You deserve beauty, love, joy, and wonder. It's okay to really live again.

THIRTEEN

Facing Fears and Befriending Death

We were able to offer our *They That Sow in Tears* workshop just once at Gerldine's garden before we had to move it to a "virtual garden" on Zoom after the COVID-19 pandemic started. With COVID came the sudden end to the psychological health that had been restored in my life during those stable middle years of rebuilding. A friend of mine refers to our collective existence prior to COVID as the "before times." And just like when Mark died, the pandemic has, for me, been a seismic "before" and "after" in my life. In the space in between both "befores" and "afters," my lizard brain took over for a few months. Another friend of mine, who I called for support during my initial psychological spin out at the onset of COVID, reminded me about the lizard brain. Lizards live with only their limbic system, he said. It's all fight, flight, feed, fear, and fornicate. The lizard's job is to survive. We agreed that lizards probably don't get to thrive. A journal entry from March 2020 gives us a look into when my reveling stopped and my lizard brain took over:

I'm self-isolated in my bedroom for the second day. It is hard to believe but we woke up one day to find the world changed by a virus. Today is March 22, 2020. We have over 15,000 cases of coronavirus now in New York State and more than 300,000 in the world! I have never known a time of such high stress and anxiety—not since the first days following Mark's death. I developed symptoms about four days ago, even though we haven't left the house for eight days. Brian is going to have to go out today for groceries and medicine for me. All I've been thinking about is the wedding, but right now, I just want to keep my children safe. I am absolutely terrified we are all going to die! I read a thread on Twitter today by an epidemiologist at Harvard. She said we may lose up to 1 million American lives! We need to prepare ourselves that someone we love will probably die from this virus. I can't; I can't go through another loss!!! No one knows how it is contracted yet but it may be respiratory? Grace may be a teenager now but every time she gets sick, even just with a cold, her asthma flares. What will happen to her if she gets this virus? What will happen to me with all of my other health problems? I can't lose anyone else. I can't! What if Brian dies before we can even get married or I am widowed a second time? What if I die and the kids are orphaned? I keep telling the kids I'm fine and we're just being cautious which is why I'm staying in my bedroom. How can this be happening! It's been six years since the last catastrophe in my life. It seems I'm due for it again.

I had let myself sail out again from the island of grief and I had been tricked into thinking the water was still. I had dared to love again and embrace life. And as has happened every other time in my life when I gave myself permission to be happy, something terrible had come along to put me in my place. I did nothing but chastise myself when COVID started and, in a very narcissistic way, I personalized a global pandemic to the hyperlocal level of my own doing. Now, a powerful undertow capsized my boat again. I'm sure every time the world has had to cope with plague and pandemic, parents and lovers worry. But never before in history were we conscious of it inching closer and closer to us every time we hit the refresh button. Anxiety would, of course, be heightened for those of us who were solo parents.

I took some relief in the fact that when the pandemic hit, I was no longer living alone with young children. There were more adults in our home than children when COVID started. I knew my anxiety would have been a thousand times worse if it was only me and the kids, as it would have been had it come just two short years earlier. Still, anxiety has been my constant companion since COVID started. The first eight weeks of the lockdown were the worst. I felt like my anxiety was spinning out of control every day.

Specifically, I thought a lot about how claustrophobic I felt when the kids and I were trapped in the house during Snowvember, just two weeks after Mark's death. Every breath I took then was focused on how to get out of the house. Ironically, at the start of COVID, my house was the one safe place protecting us from the global terror outside. I didn't handle my stress well. I drank a lot. I started reckoning with God again. All the tools in the toolbox that I had built up over the last few years felt like they were failing me now. I became a champion doom scroller, wasting hours and hours on Twitter diving deep into every scientific or crackpot article I could find about how to survive the apocalypse I was sure we were facing. My anxiety was feeding into the children's own mental health struggles. Worse still, the closer our planned wedding day came (and the closer the time to decide whether to cancel it or go through with it at home), the more I damaged my relationship with Brian. I didn't see it at the time because my lizard brain was reigning supreme, but I was pregaming the loss I was sure would come.

Somewhere between March 2020 and June 2020— when Brian and I were supposed to be wed—I had convinced myself that I was just biding my time before COVID would make me a widow again. All of the hurts from my marriage to Mark suddenly rose to the surface again. All of my hurts after his death did, too. My fear of abandonment accompanied my heartbeat. I let doubt creep in about whether marrying Brian was the right decision for me and my children.

I wasn't sure if it was that I was just granting myself permission to do whatever I needed to do to psychologically survive this time in my life or if I was running away from my choice to risk love and loss all over again by marrying Brian, but either way, I was tired of feeling powerless. This time, I unconsciously decided I would take control. If I had been steering the raft we had cobbled together with remnants from our first shipwreck, with a brain now back on high alert for more trauma, I was ready to crash the raft into smithereens so long as I was the one with the power to decide when the inevitable shipwreck would occur. The idea of destroying everything we had built together actually felt safer to me than letting go of control and giving it all over to the universe. As each day in quarantine rolled into the next, I pushed Brian further and further away. Every once in a while, I'd toss myself into the ocean again and then come up gasping for air, whispering this mantra to myself: *the world is going through a collective trauma and we can't make trauma not traumatic.* Even if no one I knew died from COVID, it was impacting us all. I would check the Faces of COVID Twitter feed multiple times a day to see how many more people were added to its list of deaths. I wasn't personally experiencing loss from COVID, but holy hell, was my grief activated by it. I wanted to escape it all. I also, actually, couldn't.

I felt like my Shadow and my healthy self were at war. I let Shadow have her way for a while but bringing her to light was unraveling the rest of me. I set a deadline for myself to decide about whether I would, in fact, marry Brian on the date we had planned. I had to work really hard to regain control of my lizard brain. I said things out loud to myself like, *grief is not new to you; you know how to do this.* I reminded myself that uncertainty about the future had been my companion for a good long while before COVID. With no therapist to turn to, I consulted my trusty oracle. Google reminded me that to survive an under-tow, you must 1. Stay calm in order to resist the process and 2. Not wear yourself out by swimming against the current.

"The most important thing is to stay afloat," said voice-activated Google in its slightly feminine, monotonous tone. All I had to do was remember again how to stay afloat. Here I was flailing about again in the ocean of my grief that COVID had triggered, and I was forgetting that the best thing to do in a crisis was to stay calm and stop being in motion.

Soon, it was the first of May, my self-imposed deadline day to make the decision of whether we would cancel our would-be wedding in five weeks. If we kept the date, we'd have to be married at home now, with our minister on Zoom, which was going to be the apparent trend that wedding season. I woke up on decision day after a very restless sleep. It was only then that I sat with the realization that the decision I was making wasn't really about whether to marry Brian on a particular day and place and time. It was whether to marry Brian at all because I was terrified of losing him, too. Just like I had to tell the kids in the early days after Mark died, I tried to quiet my panic, telling myself: *we are safe, we are safe, we are safe.* I knew that I couldn't always trust my brain. I knew my anxiety and PTSD were running wild and had been since the start of the pandemic. Then Brian came into the bedroom, handed me my coffee, and kissed me on the forehead. I let the calm flood over me and spoke my decision.

"Let's get married in the backyard, on our wedding date. Even if we can't have anyone but the kids and Dad here. Even if Reverend Michelle has to be on Zoom. Even if I can't wear my gown or you, your tux. Let's just do this for us," I told him.

As trustworthy and easygoing as ever, Brian kissed my hand and simply replied, "Okay, dear."

Our entire backyard wedding was created thanks to Amazon Prime. My lizard brain had been fed. For the next month, I shipped myself backyard-appropriate wedding dresses to try on and send back. Oodles of DIY wedding craft supplies arrived. I ordered Brian a bowtie and he watched YouTube to learn how to tie it. I wrote our super simple ceremony. So as not to outdo the eventual wedding with friends and family we still wanted to have when safe, we'd only exchange vows and rings this time around. Our baker agreed to make a mini version of our planned wedding cake and I'd pick it up the morning of the wedding. Our florist said he'd make me a flower crown to go with my newly themed forest wedding and, since he had nowhere to go, he didn't mind driving out it to me. Brian and I scouted a sweet little spot in the woods behind our house that had a picturesque view of the rolling hills. Once Brian figured out how to get Wi-Fi to work out there on a mobile hotspot, we knew where the wedding would be.

Between trying to grow our now 100+ community gardens to help keep our community fed and prepping for the wedding, the month of May flew by. My resolve was strong. I had made my decision and was ready to roll. Luckily, city hall had just reopened their offices and when we explained our situation to the clerk, she agreed to squeeze us in to pick up our license. On the Friday before the wedding, with the wedding license in hand, I teased Brian that he better give it to me to hold onto because I was more organized. He was offended, so I let him keep it.

The night before the wedding, just after I finished the last of the florals I had crafted from my own garden, I went into his home office and asked him to get me the license so I could scan it and email it to our minister. Two minutes later, I watched Brian tense as he started to nervously paw through papers on his desk and in his file cabinet. I felt my chest tighten. I felt the lizard brain tweak.

"Where is our marriage license, babe?"

"It has to be here," he said in a huff.

But it wasn't. I took over searching because I go Commando when the lizard takes over. It was nowhere to be found on his desk or in his files. As we started going through his office garbage and recycling, and then my office garbage and recycling, and then the kitchen garbage and recycling, I became more and more agitated. Then Brian found his absentee ballot for the County Executive race. I watched his Brian brain fog and un-fog and he said, "Oh my god, I think I mailed it out in place of my vote!"

"You did WHAT!" I shouted.

He explained that he must have haphazardly signed the marriage license thinking it was his absentee ballot that was also due that week for the hotly-contested County Executive race. He said he remembered stuffing something in the envelope earlier that morning and since he was now holding the ballot, it must have been the marriage license he signed instead. Before I could say another word, he ran out barefoot to the mailbox and then held his head in his hands, "It's gone. It's gone. It must have gone out in today's mail!"

He looked at me frantically, his own lizard brain now turned on. And then the words came flaming out of my mouth: "You don't want to marry me! You did this on purpose! I knew it! I knew you didn't really want me!"

For the next few hours, I raged, and Brian pleaded with me to forgive him. We tried calling the post office. We tried calling city hall. No one answered because by that time, it was after hours.

"This is the one thing we need to make the marriage legal, Brian! Otherwise, it's just a party we are having tomorrow. How could you do this!"

And as I always do when triggered by feelings of abandonment, I ran. Except there was really nowhere to go but to go for a walk around the block because there was a fucking pandemic raging that could kill you with a microscopic virus if I strayed too close to other people. I just kept muttering, "What in the actual fuck! How could this be happening?" And then I called two of my closest girlfriends. One told me I needed to calm down, that mistakes happen and that we should probably call the minister and see what she thought the options were. The other barely held back her laughter.

"I'm sorry, I'm sorry, but that is the most Brian thing ever," she said. I remained unamused and furious. I started cataloging every little hurt in our relationship to her and explained that even if this was an unconscious mistake on his part, it was clearly a signal from the Universe that we were not supposed to be wed. At least not on the day we planned.

"Ok," she said. "So then don't get married tomorrow. It's just your family coming. Everyone will understand. Or get married tomorrow with your family by your side. And then if you have to legally get remarried on Monday, do that. It's going to be okay either way."

It was not enough to stop the PTSD spiral. It wasn't just Brian's mistake. It was evidence to me that I didn't deserve happiness. That I was choosing wrong. That I was not worthy of love. My grief pendulum was in full swing. As I went back into the house, Brian followed me from room to room like a puppy. Unlike our handful of other disagreements in our relationship, this one couldn't be hidden from the kids or my father because I was twirling out of control, and we were all stuck in the house together. Grace asked us frantically why we were fighting the night before the wedding and, through his tears, Brian told her what he had done with the marriage license. To my surprise, Grace became angry at me.

"Why are you doing this? It's just a stupid piece of paper! We have a family now and you aren't going to marry him after all of this, because of a stupid mistake?" Veda said nothing but backed away slowly. My father retreated to his room. I raged some more at Brian. And just like I had done every other time we came to a crossroads in our relationship, I spat out all the reasons to him that he was wrong for me. And all the reasons someone else would probably be better for me. And as he begged me not to leave him, I spat out all the secrets I had been keeping from him since the pandemic started, including telling him I wasn't even certain I wanted to marry him anyways, so maybe this was for the best. Then we both slumped down on the ground in his now completely disheveled office and cried. When it became clear to him that I was actually having a panic attack, he held my hand and asked me to breathe with him. I took some big, deep breaths. As the warmth of his hand flowed into mine, I centered myself. I looked around and began to laugh. Brian remained concerned. I think he actually thought I might have cracked up completely at that moment.

"How can we get married without a marriage license?" I asked.

"I don't know," he said. "But I will do whatever I have to do tomorrow to make this right. I want to marry you. I love you."

"I don't deserve your love," I said. "Didn't you just hear all the terrible things I just said?"

"Yes," he said. "And I love you anyways."

And like a child who was done throwing her tantrum and was tired out by it, I said, "Fine. Go ahead and love me then." He led me down to the daybed in the sunroom, which is one of our favorite places to retreat to.

"Just let me hold you tonight and we'll figure out the rest in the morning."

"Fine," I said. And surprisingly, I fell asleep in his arms. A few hours later, he ushered me up the stairs and tucked me into bed. He laid his head down next to mine and kissed me gently. "I love you. You need to know that."

In the morning, when I woke, I looked around with fresh eyes and there he was, sleeping soundly next to me. I grounded myself in the safety of our bedroom, in the safety of our house, in the safety of our relationship and remembered that 1. Most decisions can be reversed, 2. We loved each other, 3. He was good to my children and me, 4. I deserved to be happy and Brian made me happy, 5. Brian never asked me to be anything but 100% who I was, he accepted all of me, including my shadow parts and, 6. Life is short, so live it now. I poked Brian, who was snoring away.

"Marry me today?" I inquired.

"Yes, dear," he said, as he turned over to keep sleeping. I poked him again.

"It's our wedding day. Time to get up."

"Ok, I'll make us some coffee," he grumbled, and just like that, our wedding day commenced. As we sipped our coffee, we tried calling the post office again and actually reached someone who gently informed us that there was no way to trace the envelope and, best case, someone would find it and return it once they realized what it was. We called city hall, which was closed until Monday. We called our minister who assured us the marriage would still be legal and that we had to trust in God and that everything was going to be okay. I poured out all of my anxieties to her and she listened, before responding: "I promise you; this is going to be okay. Believe it or not, Brian is not the first person to make a mistake like this. I'll call city hall on Monday, and we'll work it out. I'm a minister. They'll respect that. Besides, it's a wedding during a pandemic. I'm pretty sure the rules are arbitrary."

"Ok," I said. And then I kissed Brian deeply and he held me and told me he was sorry, that it was a mistake he made in his messy office that had more to do with his absentmindedness and disorganization than it could ever have to do with his love for me. I apologized for the things I had said and did. We sat quietly with our coffee for a while and then I said, "OK, let's do this." We gathered all our supplies, hauled them out to the forest, and set up our wedding site by ourselves.

A few hours later, the house was a bustle of activity. After three months of only seeing his parents through their glass door, they arrived in our backyard, masked and six feet apart, trying as they might to help Brian with the final preparations for our tiny, backyard wedding. The kids and I did our hair and makeup and then they went to dress. As I placed a crown of peonies on my head, I laughed at the absurdity of it all. I sat down on the bed and took out the diamond necklace Mark had given me on our wedding day.

"I love you, Mark." I told him. "You were the first love of my life, and you are the father to our children. I will love you forever. But it's time for me to let go of this fear. To let go of this feeling of unworthiness. To settle into the belief that I was not responsible for your death and that I deserve to be loved again."

Whatever anxiety I was feeling just twelve hours before had dissipated. I was about to marry again. I put away the necklace, redid my smeared makeup, and heard Grace yelling that I was about to be late for my own wedding because Brian had already started the music.

"Tell him not to worry, I'm not going to stand him up!" Then I grabbed my bouquet, pulled on my mud boots under the navy blue lace dress I had settled on, and trounced out to the backyard where the path to the forest started. My children were waiting there to escort me down the winding trail. Along with the bouquet, I held my phone in my hand and an instrumental version of Bebe Rexha's "Meant to Be" played as the kids and I linked arms and marched through the mud to meet Brian, his parents, my dad, and my youngest brother and his wife. My heart swelled with joy. Seeing the faces of the people I loved most gathered together, for the first time in months, gave me great solace. My other brother and his family, along with our minister, were cheering on Zoom. Brian cried when he saw me arrive at our chosen spot. Five minutes later, we were official-ish.

That evening, we had a catered meal from the one fine dining restaurant in town that was open. They had kindly offered to deliver it when I told them I needed dinner for nine for a quarantine wedding. We enjoyed our cake, and everyone stayed safe at their own tables. Later that night, my dad and the kids went out for ice cream. Brian and I took a bottle of champagne into the hot tub. The stars were just starting to come out. He held me close, and I relaxed again into him.

"No more secrets," he said gently.

"No more secrets," I agreed. "If you are struggling, you need to be honest with me. I can handle it. You don't have to carry all of this alone, Jeanette."

"Yes, husband," was my reply.

First thing on Monday morning, Brian called city hall, and just as our minister had said, the lady on the other side of the phone simply shook her head, clucked her tongue, and said he wasn't the first groom to lose a marriage license. An hour later, Brian had a new marriage license in hand and by day's end, we were fully legally married.

COVID-19 has been a lesson for me in living in the undertows when the water seemed still on the surface. It's been all about taming my lizard brain and learning to manage uncertainty on a grand scale. In some ways, I think being widowed helped me cope better than some people. Even though those first few months of COVID were the hardest psychologically on me and the kids, like everyone else, I adjusted over time.

Brian and I went for a lot of walks in those woods behind the house. We took it day by day. I let go of making plans for the future since so much was unknown. We rescheduled with the wedding venue and had to cancel our plans again. I painted and played piano. Brian and I honeymooned as planned in Lake Placid for a week. The COVID rates were so low in that part of the state that we even dined indoors and got proper haircuts. When harvest time finally came and went that September of 2020, and things slowed enough for me to catch my breath at work, I went back to therapy. My former therapist Alice, who had moved out of the area, was now seeing clients on Zoom, and agreed to do a few calls with me. Each Thursday that fall, I'd call her from the sanctity of my car, parked in the driveway. It was the only place in a household of five people and two dogs where I could get an hour alone. Alice helped me steady my anxiety enough to not go overboard again. I had my feet firmly planted back on the shore. Maybe because Alice was not, in fact, superhuman, or maybe because I really had become a different person in the decade that had passed since we last started therapy together, I found myself struggling to feel connected to her. After a few weeks of picking apart the anxiety that led to me almost calling off the wedding, Alice told me she thought I was doing just fine.

"Really?" I asked.

"Yes," she said, "You are okay. And quite frankly, there are people dealing with a lot more now than you are."

She was not wrong.

One of those people was my friend, Luke. Just a few months prior to the COVID lockdown, Luke and I had reconnected, sadly because he had just become widowed himself. His wife, Dana, died at the end of 2019. Their children were seventeen and twenty at the time. Luke and I went to high school together. Like people did for me, I checked in on him whenever I sensed from his social media posting that he was going through a rough time with his grief. In addition to coping with Dana's death, Luke had also been dealing with his own cancer diagnosis in the year prior to Dana's passing. His brother had also died just before Dana did. It was a lot for one person to carry. Within a year of Dana's death, Luke's cancer metastasized to his brain. Shortly after my wedding to Brian, Luke reached out and asked if there was a place for his story in this book which he knew that I was working on. He had just been released from the hospital following a seizure that caused a bad fall.

Once he was resettled at home and more stable, I invited him to video chat, and we immediately got into how hard it was for him to have to confront his own mortality so soon after Dana's death. Luke admitted he was living on borrowed time. He said, "I've had my minutes, hours, and days of just bawling like a baby. I had my time asking why am I having to go through this? Why am I going through this alone?"

Luke understood that asking these questions was part of the expected grief process. He relied heavily on his Wiccan faith. "Wicca teaches us to celebrate the life (of the deceased). I take a lot of comfort in doing just that, in celebrating Dana's life. My faith wasn't shaken, but I had to go through that process of mourning. But I also have to be able to just compartmentalize and move on to deal with all the other issues."

"Is there ever a point in which you stop compartmentalizing?" I asked.

He laughed heartily, "Never. Absolutely not."

Luke shared his fear that if he didn't work through his grief process, both in relation to Dana's death and in relation to his own, he'd end up like his brother, who drank himself to death. Luke told me that he turned to alcohol to cope for a little while but said he knew he was a "dry drunk," and that it "wouldn't end well." Instead, he chose to lean into his grief, letting himself feel all of the feelings about how shitty life had been treating him. I asked him a question then, that I hoped wasn't going too far.

"In many ways, you are dealing with what every widow and widower fears the most. Something is happening to you now and it will take you away from your kids. What do you do with that?"

"That's really the hardest one. I'm tearing up over that one right now," Luke interjected. He breathed and continued, "When we first found out the cancer had metastasized to the brain a year ago, I told my neurosurgeon, and he has heard it from me every step of the way since then: Sara, my daughter, graduates from high school in spring of 2022. That milestone is non-negotiable. I have her eighteenth birthday in 6 months and 9 days and then her graduation from high school. I live by milestones right now. I need to make it to her birthday and then I need to make it to her graduation. I'm not planning anything after that. I'm pretty confident I can make it six months. To at least not have her orphaned until she is legally an adult."

I asked him how much Sara knows about the seriousness of his illness.

"I sugar-coated it at first," he reflects. "Right up until this last bout. I can't sugar coat it anymore." He told me his greatest fear was that Sara already believed she had nothing left to live for. We talked about the steps Luke was taking to support Sara. He found her an excellent therapist and he told me that he was really trying to be present with her and talk as much as he could about her concerns. "Especially right now," he said, "I'm letting myself be vulnerable with her." Luke's adult son has autism and as Luke's prognosis became grimmer after Dana's death, Luke had to arrange to have his son moved into a group home in another city.

In July of 2021, Luke invited friends from near and far to come celebrate his life on his birthday with him while he still could. I passed on the trip because of my own fears about COVID and traveling, but I smiled as I watched his day unfold on Facebook. He had been in and out of the hospital over the past two years. There had been times he had been radio silent, which left friends worried about how to get in touch with him and how things were for him. I watched with relief when he shared the celebration for Sara's eighteenth birthday and then her accelerated graduation from high school. I've watched him use humor to cope with each worsening update about his health. His tumors are now untreatable, and one is so large it has pushed out a unicorn-horn shaped bump on his head. In true Luke fashion, he named the bump: Lumpy. Luke shares regular updates about Lumpy's adventures on #FuckCancerFridays on his Facebook feed. As his time on this earth draws nearer to an end, I see him sharing more and more about gratitude, imparting wisdom to his community on the regular about how we need to make the most of the time we have. He shares about the simple joys in life; his beloved cats that keep him calm, the hydrotherapy unit he was able to get to help him with his pain, and he asks for help when he needs it. Luke is living his remaining days whole-heartedly and with vulnerability. He also seems in a very healthy mindset for someone facing the end. I remembered what Debbie Ford said in her writings about suffering and acceptance: "To transcend our suffering, we must go against our instinct to hold on and instead surrender to the path of letting go."[31]

I wonder if I would have the courage to do the same if I was the one facing my own death within two years of being widowed. I pray for Luke and his children. When he leaves this earth, I hope it is with the dignity he needs, that it is at home, with his children, his cats, and his friends.

When we surrender to what is happening only in the present moment; when we surrender our ideas of what should be for what is, we can embrace change in the moment and that can change the course of our lives, for however long we live them. I am grateful for friends like Luke and a partner like Brian, who remind me to not let fear steer my ship.

---

31 Ford, *Spiritual Divorce,* 2006, 44.

Lessons Learned:
How to Make Big Decisions in Spite of Your Lizard Brain

While you will hear the adage, "Don't make any big decisions when grieving" from everyone, the fact of the matter is that you will have to make a lot of decisions, big and small, after loss. Some of these decisions start immediately, such as deciding whether to donate your partner's organs, or how to honor them through a celebration of life. Then there are the decisions involved in the "business" of death: what to do about joint bank accounts, credit cards to cancel or defer, whether to apply for Social Security Insurance benefits for your kids or to tap into retirement savings early to help you get by. As your life moves forward, your widowed brain will be bombarded with other decisions that must be made. The most important are the decisions that let you create a life you will love. Here's a few things to remember that hopefully will help:

1. **Most decisions are reversible.** Sure, selling the home you lived in with your late spouse is a huge decision. What if you sell it and regret it? What if your new house turns into a money pit? There are a million things we can conjecture about all the ways things can go wrong when we have to make a decision. Instead of denying this, embrace it. Write a list of the pros and cons about the question at hand. Then choose the top three worst cons. Write out the worst-case scenarios for each of them. Short of your own death as the worst-case scenario, really look at whether the scenarios could be changed or influenced. If you are worried that buying a new house in an unfamiliar neighborhood could lead you to buyer's remorse and you'd sell again within a few months, so be it. Challenge yourself to plot alternative endings to the worst-case scenario.

2. **Trust your gut.** This is a "both/and" situation. You cannot know the ending AND you can still make a decision. BOTH things can be true AND you can always change your mind. But you can also listen to that voice inside you that is propelling you in one direction or the other. That voice told me two weeks after Mark died, as my garage roof crumbled on his man cave in a literal metaphor of what my November 2014 was going to be like, that I could not maintain

the rambling old house by myself. So, I plotted alternative endings, including having my father move in with us or getting a roommate, or getting a home inspector to tell me exactly what was wrong with it and how much it would cost to hire contractors to fix all the problems. But at the end of the day, the decision was a practical one as much as it was an emotional one. For the nine months we stayed in the house after his death, it was an empty shell of what it once had been and even what my reimagined plans for it had been when I thought about living my life with the kids there independent of Mark. None of those options seemed emotionally feasible for me anymore. I knew I needed to start over. When it comes to your decision point, listen to your first thought, as well as your most persistent thoughts about it.

3. **Sometimes we have to make decisions about people, not things.** Trust is often shattered when we've lived through loss, especially if the loss was violent, sudden, or involved any drama with others still alive. When our trust is eroded in people or processes, it's invaluable to get second and third and fourth opinions. What does your best friend think about the new person you want to introduce your kids to? What do your widowed-people peers (because we all need some of those) say about selling your wife's prized possession? If you have someone older than you (and/or younger than you) that you trust, get their opinions. Sometimes people's opinions will hurt and sometimes you will choose to do what you need to do regardless. Take opinions for what they are. If you are in therapy, your therapist can be an objective ear that can help you process what to do and how to do it.

4. **If you have the luxury of time, take it slow.** It can be really easy to rush into action when we feel pulled to escape reality. I knew within a week of losing my job that I was going to have to decide about moving in with Brian, but it was a six-month process to actually do so.

5. **If you do not have the luxury of time and you have to make a fast decision, seek counsel from those you trust or just go with your gut decision.** More often than not, you know what you need.

6. **Break down big decisions into more manageable chunks.** If you hate your job and want to leave it immediately, can you plot out a path to do so? What would have to happen first? Are there ways to make the situation more tolerable while you are in the "waiting place?" For example, can you speak with your supervisor about taking a leave of absence or transferring to another department or location? When I was first widowed, I surprised myself by asking my boss to work at home part-time and I was even more surprised when she said yes (this was back before we all had to work at home during COVID).

7. **If you are contemplating any decision that will greatly affect your finances, seek professional advice.** I had almost no money left to my name, besides the equity in the house, when Mark died. But I swallowed my pride and saw a financial advisor for the first time in my life. She helped me figure out how to pay the mortgage and afford term life insurance so that the kids would be protected financially if anything happened to me. This was a huge weight off my shoulders. When Brian and I moved in together, we consulted a lawyer to help us figure out how to set up our new home so that we would be better protected individually if either of us died while jointly listed on the mortgage, prior to being married. Professional advisors are professional for a reason. Seek their counsel. You don't have to know all the things.

PART V

Sailing Out Again

FOURTEEN

My Children's Grief Over Time

So much has changed in my children's lives since that fateful day their father died. They have moved twice, changed school districts, grown up from little girls into young adults with thoughts and opinions all of their own. When Grace was 15, she came out as bisexual. A year later, when Veda was 12, she disclosed she was unsure of her gender identity, surprising neither me nor her sister. As I always have, I welcomed my children to step fully into themselves, also knowing that the teen years are meant to reckon with identity in all kinds of ways. Veda is now Milo and for the remainder of this book, I will honor Milo's request to use their chosen name and pronouns (they/them) from the time of their transition in my story. Change has been a constant in Milo's life. Milo half-joked with me one day about why I hadn't asked them to tell their story for my book. So, I invited them to sit down for an interview. Seated comfortably in the big chair in my office, Milo began to share unprompted.

"What I remember about Dad was that he was a lot of fun. Chaotic too! That must be where I get my chaotic energy from!" I asked Milo to tell me a story about Mark and Milo shared an early memory of how they couldn't sleep at nap time one day, so Mark said they better go to sleep or they would get farted on. We both laughed. I asked them for other warm and fuzzy-type memories, and they talked about when Mark came to their kindergarten classroom and wowed everyone with his juggling skills. Like many young children who experience loss, Milo talked about the confusion that surrounded Mark's sudden death.

"I was only five," Milo said sadly. I summoned my courage, then, and asked Milo to tell me about the day their father died. There was a long pause, and then Milo said, "I was really confused and sad. I don't really know what happened that day. I was waiting for you to come back to me and to tell me what was going on. You didn't come back. Later, you told us he wasn't with us anymore. I didn't cry. I was just confused. I remember I had his picture. That's all I remember."

We talked then about how confusing it was for Milo to watch Mark have seizures and not understand what was happening; how confusing it was that Mark and I had separated but still spent time together every week as a family; how confusing it was to have to pick up and change schools and homes within a year of Mark's death, right after Milo finished kindergarten. Throughout our discussion, Milo returned to the word *confused* to describe this time in their life. Psychologist William Worden posited that most young children had a hard time articulating the meaning of a parent's death or telling the story in a straight line. Worden said that children described an emptiness that seemed almost bottomless shortly after their parent's death.[32] Such was the case for Milo.

"It was really strange at first," Milo said, remembering those first days, weeks, and months. "I didn't know this new neighborhood or where we were in the world. I know we didn't want to be in that house (the home we shared once with Mark) anymore. It's also kind of strange because you're always worried about what will happen next."

I asked Milo what the term *separation anxiety* meant to them as it's a term that's been used a lot in our house. "I was so worried something would happen to you because something happened to him. What if I lost you too?"

Not all the things about the new house were bad though. Milo jumped to their beloved magnolia tree, then.

---

32 Worden, "The Four Tasks of Mourning." June 6, 2013.

"I'd go up there for hours of the day. It was my place to just be," they said in a voice much older than their twelve years. Milo continued, "I used to talk to the tree a lot. I don't know, I like talking to things that don't talk back."

Milo and I agreed that trees are good listeners. I recalled then how the tree was another loss for Milo. Milo reminded me how after selling the new house we found out its new owners cut down all the trees, including the beautiful magnolia, the gorgeously-perfumed lilac, and even the towering pine.

Milo said mournfully, "I wanted to buy that house again someday. I thought I'd live there again because that was my favorite tree."

"Bastards!" I exclaimed with a fist shake and we giggled.

Milo, who has a love of nature as big as my own, then said, "It was really my favorite plant in the whole world." I reminded Milo of how, on the day we moved out of that little house in the village and into our new home with Brian, Milo took a few buds and leaves from that magnolia tree with them so they could remember our "healing house."

"Why did you call it our healing house, Milo?"

"It was just that," they said. "We could be with ourselves there in that house and focus on our healing. The tree healed me. Buddy, our puppy, did too. He'd climb onto me if I was sad and just snuggle me."

Milo and I talked about the people who supported us, how difficult Milo still found the anniversaries of Mark's death, as well as Christmases and birthdays to be. We talked about Brian coming into my life and how Milo had to adjust to having him in their life as well. Then the ways our lives changed again when we three moved in with Brian, got our second dog, and the pandemic came crashing down on our stability.

"Oh, that big stressful thing!" Milo joked when I pointed out how they failed to recall that global-turned-local change in their life. "I got a lot of stress when we had to go into quarantine with the pandemic. It's another trauma."

Trauma rolled off all of our tongues with ease as the kids have had it in their vernacular for years by this point in time. I asked Milo what *trauma* meant to them.

"I guess it means something happens to you, like bad things you think will only happen to other people but then they happen to you." I started to change the subject, but Milo interjected. "Wait, I want to go back to that. The thing is, because of the trauma, I'm more mature than other people; than my friends. They don't know what trauma is, really, even if they think they know. They don't know what *this all* is like."

Even though I provided my children early access to the best therapists in town, it did not prevent Milo from developing pretty severe post-traumatic stress disorder. I told Milo I was sorry that trauma forced its way into their childhood and how I wished more than anything it hadn't.

"It definitely changed my childhood," Milo said, their voice shaking. We both started tearing up. Milo then detailed the ways in which they felt a loss of control in their life. Milo's voice cracked and their bottom lip quivered. "I'm always thinking about who is next. The next bad thing."

We talked about the reliving that happens with PTSD and what triggered Milo's trauma response in their body.

"I get triggered by a lot of things now: sirens, ambulances, definitely blood. I don't know why, but I don't like blood that much. I've grown out of it a bit, but I used to really worry about it. I remember seeing him (Mark) being loaded in (to the ambulance) and the police coming." Milo has maintained this in all of their therapy over the years: the belief that they watched Mark come out on a gurney and get loaded into the ambulance and taken to the hospital, even though that never happened as Mark had already passed by the time we found him and his body stayed at the apartment for hours after Milo had left with their sister. Confusion clouded all of our memories of that day. I began to cry harder then, thinking about my baby sitting in the car, waiting for me to bring word of whatever horrible thing was happening inside. Tears streamed down as I considered the chaos Milo must have felt with all of the police and ambulance on the scene, with no one but a stranger, the apartment's cleaning lady, to attempt to comfort them until family arrived.

In *A Parent's Guide to Raising Grieving Children*, authors Silverman and Kelly explain that for a child, a sudden death of a parent is like having the core of them ripped away. Their whole life changes in the space of one sentence being uttered.[33] Like many school-age children who are grieving, Milo's separation anxiety was generally better while occupied by the tasks of school but worse at certain points throughout the day. I recalled how angry I was at Milo's third grade teacher for calling me in for a conference to tell me that Milo needed more help than I must have been giving as Milo was "taking attention away" from the other children by standing in front of the windows at the end of the day, their little face pressed to the glass, searching for whether I would be there as promised at dismissal.

We returned to therapy for help with Milo's separation anxiety. Milo recalled this experience this way: "The first time in therapy, I didn't get it that much. I was just supposed to close my eyes and think about things but it was so confusing."

Once I switched Milo from the child psychologist they originally saw to Elizabeth Davis' trauma-specific practice and they started working with a new therapist there, things improved. Milo was able to work through a lot of anger about our separation and Mark's death using play therapy and they learned how to verbalize their feelings and body sensations. Then COVID-19 hit and seemingly undid two years of progress. Milo's stomach aches worsened to constant pain. Their weight dropped by almost 30 pounds, to a very dangerous level. Milo was terrified for me to leave the house after the official lockdown ended and summer forced my return to work in the city's community gardens. For Milo, every time I left the house during the pandemic, the belief was that I would not come home to them. I wasn't sure if Milo's weight loss and stomach pain were a symptom of the anxiety or a physical illness.

Once the lockdown lifted enough to get Milo in to see a doctor, blood work revealed that Celiac disease could be the culprit. Milo's anxiety about medical procedures, which they also associated with Mark's death in some way, would have to be dealt with so Milo could undergo an endoscopy. I thought medication might be needed to help keep Milo's anxiety symptoms under control, but I was hesitant to start down the medication pathway given all the ways it can

---

33 Phyllis Silveman and Madelyn Kelly, *A Parent's Guide to Raising Grieving Children,* (Oxford University Press, 2009), 60-61.

affect a young person's brain, and how psychiatric meds played out in Mark's health story. So back to therapy we went again.

Milo continued their story, "This year, when I did EMDR, it was really different. It worked!"

It certainly did. Milo went from being paralyzed by fear at the idea of a medical procedure to getting through their endoscopy at peak COVID in June 2020 like a champ. An official diagnosis of Celiac disease followed, along with a newly regimented eating plan and work with a nutritionist to get Milo back to a healthy weight. Therapy (now on Zoom) helped Milo so much that by the time they entered seventh grade, they were able to stay home alone for up to two hours at a time and felt prepared to come home to an empty house while we worked out-of-the-home and Grace stayed at school for extracurricular activities.

Milo's courage and strength amaze me still. At the time of our interview, at the tender age of twelve, Milo had survived the losses of their grandmother and father, moving and changing schools within the year of his death, moving again when Brian and I wanted to blend into our family, a global pandemic, a diagnosis of Celiac disease and a scary loss of thirty pounds because of that, a strict food regimen to recover, starting middle school, and questioning their sexual and gender identities.

"Milo, what gives you the inner strength to not only get through these difficult things, but to come out as kind to people as you are?"

Spoken like a true old soul, Milo said, "They say that when you've had trauma, you come out kinder. Because you've been through it, and you don't want other people to go through that." Tears started streaming down Milo's face. "Losing Daddy was just the hardest."

I nodded my head in agreement. "What do you want other kids to know about grief, Milo?"

"I want them to know that you get better over time. It's confusing at first, but you'll get better at coping with it. Everyone has anxiety here and there, but my anxiety has definitely gotten a lot better today than even two years ago. I think you did a pretty good job, Mom."

I sniffled and let it sink in that my kid was going to be alright.

"If you could tell your Daddy anything right now, what would you want him to know about you?" I asked.

Milo didn't hesitate to answer: "That I'm following in his footsteps. I like to dress like him a lot. I'm trying to play his guitar, but I failed at it. This year, I thought about my identity a lot. I had an identity crisis during quarantine. And I came out (as gay and transgender) and you've supported me by using my pronouns and buying me all my pride stuff." Milo and I reminisced about attending their first Pride festival that past summer together. "And now this year, since I have less anxiety about being by myself and about myself, I joined the GSA (Gender-Sexuality Alliance) at my school and we talk about other kids like me. And I'm excited because we did Socktober this month to help LGBTQ kids who are homeless, and I might even be in the news about it! I feel happier now that I came out, and my grief feels a little less because now I know who I am."

I told Milo that their father absolutely would be proud of them.

"I'm never going to forget about him. Whenever I'm sad or worried about you or myself, I ask him to be with me."

I then posed my last question to Milo: "What advice do you have to give parents of grieving kids?"

Milo thought about it for a minute and looked me straight in the eye and said, "You just need to give us time to get a handle on everything."

Milo the Brave, I have christened them. A reminder to them of how strong they are in the face of their fears. A reminder to myself that if my children can live their lives in the face of such great loss and difficult emotion, so can I. So many of my early worries for them after their father's death were about how greatly his death would impact their mental health. My own traumas from childhood have been a specter accompanying me through every phase of my development and I know this shall too for them. The difference being that my children were given access to all of the tools and skills and people they needed to hopefully help them cope with the shipwreck, with the long swim to safety, and with their eventual return to the water.

It's important for widowed parents to not lose sight of the myriad ways our children's grief will change shape over time. As Milo said, they will carry it with them forever. Tuning into what your child needs at each age and stage of development is important. Sometimes it can be hard to figure out if an issue with your child is from the impact of their grief or is just part of the normal trajectory of a child's development. This is what I wanted to learn more about from Dr. Julie Kaplow, a clinical psychologist and currently the Executive Director of The Trauma and Grief Center at The Hackett Center for Mental Health in Houston, Texas. During the last few years that I worked as a curriculum developer, I became connected to some folks at the National Child Traumatic Stress Network. A few years after Mark died, they asked if I would serve on their work group for bereaved parents. This is how I met Julie and came to learn about her new multidimensional theory of grief in children.

Julie, along with her colleagues Bob Pynoos and Christopher Layne, have formulated this theory based on how children cope and adapt to different bereavement-related challenges. When I told Julie I was writing my memoir on parenting through loss, she offered to sit down and tell me more about their theory. Over the last two decades, Julie and her colleagues have been studying how grief manifests in children and their work supports the idea that children usually grapple with three main dimensions of grief: 1) *separation distress*—the yearning and longing children carry for their deceased parent; 2) existential or *identity distress*—how will the child live their life without the deceased parent and 3) *circumstance-related distress*—a preoccupation with how their parent died and grappling with their feelings of whether they could have intervened to prevent death. Julie said, "Kids can experience these challenges in either healthy, adaptive ways or unhealthy ways. For example, the way we define *adaptive grief* in the context of separation distress is finding healthy ways of connecting to the person who died, such as engaging in activities that the person used to enjoy, or holding onto cherished memorabilia from that person." Julie went on to detail that children with adaptive grief may strive to live the legacy of the person who died, so they focus on fulfilling the goals and dreams of the person who died or wanting to live the life they think their parent would have wanted for them. Julie said that when a child is grappling with circumstance-related distress they often focus on how they can transform the circumstances into something meaningful that can help others not suffer in the same way. I asked her to tell me more. She told me the story of a nine-year-old child whose father died in a plane crash and how that child, even at such an early age, was determined to be a mechanical engineer so he could rectify such engineering failures in the future. Julie also noted that childhood grief research was very much still in its infancy and that the application of adult models of bereavement did not necessarily apply to children, hence her research. That said, she and her colleagues have been able to validate what psychologist William Worden first discovered in the early 1990s when he conducted his Child Bereavement Study: the vast majority of children who lose a parent, maybe even as high as ninety percent of bereaved children, will go on to function just fine over time. This is not to say that children aren't greatly impacted by the loss, but in terms of their mental health and displayed behaviors, they grow into adults who are perfectly okay. However, about ten percent of children who lose a parent will struggle so much that they could benefit from more significant clinical intervention with a professional. Julie told me that many of the children she sees in the grief clinic where she worked and conducted her research are brought in by a concerned parent. She said in most cases, the child's symptoms are normal for the experience of loss they are coping with. In those cases, they'll refer the family to a community bereavement support program that typically offers peer support, but not see the child in therapy. She noted that in many cases, clinical symptoms related to maladaptive grief are not seen until at least one year after the death, when the permanency of it really settles onto the child. Julie explained, "I think oftentimes this is also when social support disappears for the family." Julie shared about how the New York Life Foundation did a study where they surveyed 1,000 adults who lost a parent as a kid and what they heard was that the social support tapered off within three months. When researchers inquired how long the participants would have wanted that support as a child, the answer was for at least six years. Julie continued: "They are calling it the *grief gap*, where you are just sort of alone in it as the surviving parent and kids feel that too. And because our society still has so many issues in talking about death and how to support kids when they are grieving, it creates a veil of silence."

I count my children and I, then, as some of the lucky ones. While our social support network has changed over time, the friends who supported me and the children early in our bereavement, by and large, are still in our lives, even if not at their previous level of involvement. Those who have remained closest to us made sure that whenever I felt overwhelmed or worried about the children, that they would be there for them too, whether for a quick text check in or a fun day out to distract my kids from the weight of the world on their little shoulders. Julie and I talked about another key question of her research: when do we know children have healed? She said, "We don't like to use the term 'healed' because, to some degree, no one ever completely 'heals' after the death of a loved one, and we don't want to set that expectation. Instead, we talk about grief changing over time and gaining more tools to cope with it. We have seen children learn to make meaning from the death and begin to understand the ways in which the experience shaped them into the person they are today, including some of their most important and admirable traits." She told me one more story then, of a child who was the sole survivor of a tragedy in which everyone else in the family was killed. This child said to her, "As much as I would never wish this on anyone and I'm not glad that it happened, I know it has made me who I am." "Children can get there," Julie concluded, "eventually, with the right support."

Earlier, I wrote about learning that there is more than one type of kid grief. I want to share my other child's story with you now, in her own words. When I interviewed Grace on New Year's Day 2022, she was almost seventeen. She had survived seven-and-a-half years without her father. Grace and I started off with the mixed feelings she had about attending Mark's memorial services and my decision for her not to see her father's body after his death.

"It didn't feel real. I feel like it would have made it real to see him. I wanted to see his face and I didn't understand why I wasn't allowed to." Grace said she feels like I made the right choice, looking back on my decision, because she wouldn't have wanted the memory of Mark's bruised face to be her last memory of him. She talked with an almost philosophical air about the way her life could have been different if he had lived.

"We probably would have stayed in that house on Lake, and I would have gone to Frontier (school district), and my life would be different than it is now.

I'd be a whole different person with different experiences with different people."

Grace relayed that she felt his death gave her a deep understanding of people. "He was compassionate, and he taught me that," she continued. "And I try to pass that onto others like I think he would want me to do."

Grace shared that she had to "grow up fast" as she didn't have her other parent to parent her and she felt like she had to fill that void a bit.

"I think I overstepped a bit. I thought I had to be independent. Like it was my job to do that to help you. I feel like I did lose my childhood in Blasdell (the village we were living in when Mark died), but then I did get a bit of childhood back when we moved to Hamburg and I had kids around me and could just play the day away."

Grace and I talked about how she put up no resistance to the move. She cracked a smile.

"Sometimes the best thing to do with you, Mom, is just to agree with you." Her tone turned serious, "I think I needed that change though. I was stuck. Blasdell was where all the bad stuff happened to me. I assumed getting away from there would help us, even though I was sad to leave my friends and my school. But it was an exciting new adventure and I'm always up for an adventure."

I trusted that Grace wasn't just saying these things to make me feel better. Grace genuinely perceived the world around her, even in and after our loss, as a world in which the glass was always half-full. Whereas my youngest child loathed me for making us move and ripping further stability away, my oldest child geared up for the ride. Grace agreed with Milo's assessment of the small house we downsized to in the first three years after Mark's death.

"That little house gave us a space to heal, before we could really pick ourselves up and move on."

As we reflected on her experience of grief across the ages, Grace said studiously, "In the beginning, I had no concept of what that term, *grief*, meant. But I started going to therapy and that was weird for me at first. I didn't want to talk to this random lady about my feelings and I didn't want to show that vulnerable side of myself. I wasn't even sure what I was feeling at that time."

Grace explained she just didn't have the words to express what was going on inside. Eventually, she came to enjoy going, as there was a giant playroom and it was easy for her to be distracted by the toys. As time went on, she started to understand that she could talk about her feelings in therapy. "The feelings would come in waves over the years. At nine, I didn't know how to feel. But by eleven, I started figuring it out a little bit and by thirteen, I was sad and maybe angry."

Grace detailed how it was hard to tell people her father was dead, especially other kids. "Now I just say, 'Oh, he's gone' and I brush it off like it's nothing but even that, it's a lot for other people, other kids to hear. And I don't like to put that on them unless they know it's coming, unless they ask." Grace always puts others' needs before her own, sometimes to her detriment. We talked about her most recent return to therapy then, at fifteen, when the pandemic started. "That's when it got really hard. The therapy sessions were all about really digging in and I felt really overwhelmed a lot of the time. But it helped. It made me really break into those feelings and dig them apart."

Grace thought that the feelings weren't different maybe than earlier, but they were bigger, and she could break them apart more and look at them. "I was angry. And in other ways, I was just accepting it. I was also sad; it was something that will always be a big negative part of my life. So, I had to learn to see it in more than one way. In seeing him in multiple ways."

I asked Grace to tell me more: What did it mean to see her dad in multiple ways? I reflected on how I had come to accept the complexities of who Mark was. I wondered if she viewed him the same way.

Grace responded, "I think I saw him through a kid's eyes. The silly, fun Dad who wanted to do all the fun things and not the adult things quite yet. Who wanted to be rough and tough and play silly with me. And then I started to realize that he wasn't always the person I thought he was. He could make really stupid decisions, and not be a grown up and place being a grown up on me a little bit. And that was hard to process. Like, oh, he did *that*?" She paused here, thoughtfully, and somewhat somberly. She told me how she was sometimes mad at him for not always doing what was best for her and what was best for him. "People have two sides to them, they all do. So, I had to accept that he wasn't the perfect Dad I thought he was. Humans make mistakes. And that's what happened."

Grace and I talked about what she's learned about herself from this loss.

"Patience, it gave me patience. But everything in my life has been about learning patience. Being patient with myself because of my medical issues, being patient with myself because of my grief, having to be patient with him. Being patient with the way his family has handled their grief. I've had to be patient, but things eventually all work themselves out."

Grace said that losing Mark made her feel very close to me and Milo.

"When you have trauma, it bonds you in a way." She talked about not understanding Milo's grief, though, as it was so different from her own. "Yes, we shared that experience, but their grief and how they have handled it has been so different from my own. We butted heads a lot because we didn't understand the other's way of grieving."

Grace reflected on how difficult it was for her that Milo was so "possessive" of me and because of Milo's separation anxiety, we often didn't go out if Milo was overwhelmed. We shifted into a discussion about secondary losses and milestone days that have been hard on her.

"Father's Day is hard but what's harder is those big days that I already know he'll miss."

Grace broke down into tears. I asked her if she wanted to stop, but she pushed my hand away and wiped her tears. She told me she thought too much about the future. How he wouldn't be there when she got her driver's license. Or her graduation. Or the day she leaves for college.

"He's not going to be there to pick me up when I fall or to see me on my wedding day. And yes, I have people who can but it's not the same. It's really hard to talk about all the ways he'll be absent. I know when those experiences happen, they'll be hard. Sometimes all you want is your dad. And you want him to hold you and rock you back and forth."

By this point in the interview, Grace and I both had tears streaming down our faces, so I stopped, and she let me hold her hand and breathe through our emotions together. One day, Grace was being held by her dad, whenever she needed it. And literally overnight, her dad was gone. She was never held by him again, laid eyes on him again, told him she loved him or heard his "I love you, Gracie girl" again. In our interview, Grace so eloquently demonstrated how quickly and also how slowly she had to come to terms with the world, as she knew it, ending. On the one hand, she talked about feeling the need to protect me by trying to fill adult shoes and getting okay quickly with things changing, such as the move and shifting schools. And on the other hand, she's done the slower work of digging deep into her emotions and processing this great loss over time.

As we neared the end of the conversation, I asked Grace what parts of Mark live on in her and she perked up.

"I have his go-go-go spirit. His musical talent. My music helps me cope and losing him gave me the strength to put so much of myself into my performances. I give them my all because I'd want him to be proud of me."

For Grace, these secondary losses of family structure, attention, and the special role her father played in her life as her key support person, are central. Mark was so many things to Grace, including being her primary partner for activities.

Grace's deepest fear is the same as Milo's. They are both waiting for the other shoe to drop: who will die next and what if it's their mother or one of them?

"Death, I'm afraid of death. It's a scary thought. It's scary to think of others dying. I'm not ready to do it all again. I know I'm going to have to someday, and that's the scary part. You're so used to this person and then they're gone," she said.

Grace shifted then to talking about how, just as she got used to the idea of Mark being gone, I went and introduced Brian into their lives. Choking back more tears, Grace seemed to drop the very adult poise she had held during most of the interview. Her face got a little pouty and her voice a little more dramatic.

"I know that Brian wasn't replacing him, but it's really hard, it's been really hard for me. I have a hard time bonding with Brian because I never felt quite attached or connected to him like I thought I should have."

Grace relayed that she didn't want to have to get close to someone new again: "I appreciate Brian a lot and I love him, but it's hard. I'm happy that you're happy and that you got married. But it's just hard to find a bond with him. It's hard for me to bond with a lot of people. I have a lot of triggers and stuff I'm afraid of."

We let that settle on us and Grace teased me through her tears that she was having a really good day before I had come along with my interview questions and messed it up. She insisted, though, that she wanted to see it out.

My last question for her was the same I had asked Milo: "What do you want newly widowed parents to know, Grace, about being a grieving child?"

Grace let out a long sigh and steeled her face, before saying: "If they're young (children), you need to help them. It's going to be hard to explain this to a kid because grown-ups don't even understand this. But you'd be surprised by how much they can take this in and handle."

She added, "Keep them connected to their friends. Give them the time and space they need to process this and then give them the resources to work through it. Just be there. Don't separate yourself from them. You need to be there with them." As if stressing this point especially, she continued emphatically: "Help them understand it and then help them understand it again when their grief changes, because it's going to change from when they're little to when they're older. You have to be there for every step of it. It's not a one-year thing. You've got to work through it with them."

We concluded with Grace, back in her near-adult brain and poise, telling me that she wanted a future when she can help people break down their grief and be a support for them, so that in doing so, she can help herself.

My children survived their loss, just as I did, by putting one foot in front of the other. As parents, we have to accept that we have both immense control and immense lack of control when it comes to our children's grief trajectory as they age and grow. Grace the Kind, Milo the Brave, and Jeanette the Wiser are on the hero's journey. The hero's origin story almost always starts with a loss; usually a profoundly traumatic one at that. Then there is an adventure, often fraught with challenges and circumstances that forces the hero to learn a lesson and win a victory with the newfound knowledge so when the hero finally returns home, they have been transformed. As Grace pointed out, we may have all had the same general experience of Mark's death, but our paths are each our own. Part of my path has been reckoning with what I can't influence on theirs and having to watch from the sidelines while they have struggled to swim to shore or dip their toes back into the ocean. This was an odyssey we were on: each of us and all of us.

One of the other clinicians I met during my time as a consultant with the bereaved parents' working group with the National Child Traumatic Stress Network was Dr. Jill Harrington. Jill wrote a book entitled *Superhero Grief: The Transformative Power of Loss,* and like all of the superheroes she discusses in the book, her own transformation story came by way of loss: she is the surviving mother to two children who lost their father when they were six and ten. Although she was a social worker and grief therapist prior to being widowed, her perspective on what we need to do to survive and thrive has changed as a result of her personal experience.

In the introduction to her book, Jill writes that grief becomes transformative when it offers grieving people the opportunity to create a "new self-narrative" and that if we let grief bend us, break us, and rebuild us, it will be our greatest teacher. "At the points at which we break, we are required to find the deepest of our strengths to heal."[34] Jill's book is written primarily for therapists and other clinicians working with bereaved families, but there is much that can be learned by surviving parents and caregivers.

It was from Jill that I first learned about the television series, *WandaVision.* We had purchased Disney+ during COVID lockdown to try to make our lives at home a happy escape and so when I learned about *WandaVision* from Jill in January 2021, I told the kids we were going to sit down as a family and watch a show together about superheroes and grief. The kids were not amused.

---

34 Jill Harrington, Robert A. Neimeyer, and Darcy Harris, eds., *Superhero Grief: The Transformative Power of Loss.* (Routledge Press), xxxiv.

"Listen, I heard this show has a Scarlet Witch in it and she's a badass confronting her loss and slaying her demons. Watch it with me, please. It's for my research."

The kids gave me the usual side-eye I get with any such sentence that ends with "it's for my research" but with nowhere to go and a pizza on the way, they agreed to watch one episode with me and Brian. One episode turned into the binge watch of all three episodes that had been released to that date. After that, we ordered pizza every Friday night for the next six weeks, eagerly awaiting the next episode drop. I could tell you nothing of *Avengers: End Game* or the Marvel Cinematic Universe (Brian, on the other hand, has lots to say about it) in which we learn Wanda's origin story. In *WandaVision*, we meet Wanda, aka the Scarlet Witch, in her perfect suburban happiness and it is only as the series unfolds that we learn she is in such deep denial over her reality that she created a whole alternate world. (Spoiler alert: skip to the next chapter if you don't want to know what's what with Wanda!).

The truth is that Wanda's beloved superhero synthetic husband, Vision, is dead and their children do not exist outside of this altered reality she creates to comfort herself. During the nine Emmy-winning episodes, we watch Wanda grapple with the tension between her past, present, and future; with longing for the real Vision, with trying to control every aspect of what is happening to her family; with reaching her breaking point, and learning how truly powerful her Chaos Magic is, even though those powers are not being used for good anymore. It is only in facing Vision's death that Wanda also is forced to reckon with the other traumas from her childhood that made her the powerful witch she is.

All of us resonated with Wanda's grief and longing. Our family had deep, deep conversations about our grief while watching *WandaVision*. I don't think there was a dry eye in the house during the last two episodes. We talked about the powers we have to either deny reality or accept the pain; the ways in which we all have tried to keep Mark's vision alive, and the ways in which our anger and our fears have held us captive.

Wanda is convinced that if she allows the truth of her loss in, if she accepts it, she will die from the pain. In the second to last episode, the faux Vision she has created to carry on the lie of her life and of her joy, confronts Wanda about the truth and Wanda finally admits to her pain. He asks her a most poignant question, "What is grief, if not love persevering?"[35]

This is the lesson we learn on the hero's journey. Grief is love persevering. And like Wanda, we, ourselves, and our children, must learn to internalize our loved ones and carry them forward in the voyage of our lives yet to be lived.

35 Schaefer, Jac, creator. *WandaVision*. Season 1, episode 8, "Previously On." Directed by Matt Shakman, featuring Paul Bettany, Elizabeth Olsen, and Kathryn Hahn. Aired February 26, 2021. Original TV Mini-series, Disney+, 2021.

Lessons Learned:
Supporting Children's Evolving Grief Over Time

In the beginning of our loss, my work as a parent was to find my children some immediate support to help them make sense of the ways in which our world changed overnight. It took us about a year and a half to move from crisis to some kind of "new normal." And then there were multiple years in which we focused on confronting the deeper pieces of our grief which were held as secrets to be unlocked. The tips that follow are practices I found useful in helping my kids navigate the map of their loss over time until they found their way back home to themselves.

1. **If you're worried about your kids, whether in the beginning or five years down the road from the initial loss, get a professional mental health assessment and if needed, get your kids into therapy.** Your local crisis center or bereavement group should be able to refer you to clinicians in your area who can meet with you and your child(ren) to assess what level of support they need. If your child needs to see a therapist, don't just take the first one with an opening. Finding a good therapist that is the right match for your child may take a few sessions. If the fit doesn't feel right after a few sessions, go find someone else, even though it will be hard on all to start over and can be costly. All the research about therapeutic impact shows that it's about finding the right therapist— more so than the type of therapy someone is engaged in—that is most beneficial. Explain to your child that they are going to therapy not because they are bad or did anything wrong but because the world did something wrong to them. Their parent died and that is too much for a kid to have to handle on their own. Say it as simply as "a therapist is a helper who can help us make sense of our feelings, including our anger and our sadness."

2. **Little kids will become big kids. Big kids can start to process their grief at deeper levels.** Just because your little kid seems "over it" doesn't mean that their levels of grief and grief-related behaviors won't shift over time. Be prepared because supporting their grief is

going to be your job for the rest of their childhoods and likely in their adult lives too.

3. **Connect your kids to other kids who have experienced parental loss.** One of the things that helped my kids most was meeting other kids in a family grief support group. I don't think they remember much about the work we did as a family in those six weeks of support sessions, but they do remember the children they made fast friends with. Your children need to know they are not an anomaly.

4. **Don't assume your teens don't want to talk about their grief anymore.** If your teens (or, really, your kids at any age) don't want to talk to you about their grief, try having them text you about it. If that doesn't work, try to find another adult who can reach them and don't take it personally. Our kids want to protect us from their pain. They don't want to be a burden and they worry that we can't handle any more than we are already handling. Sometimes they're right. Call on your village for help. If you don't have a village, seek out some new relationships, even if you're exhausted. We are not meant to carry all of this alone.

5. **Make meaning together and follow their lead.** It's been eight and a half years since Mark died. Some of the traditions and rituals we started in the beginning, we've silently let go of over the last few years. Last year, on the anniversary of his death, it was only when we were standing graveside that we remembered we were supposed to bring Mark our handwritten love notes on pumpkins as we had done every year prior. But we've kept up our Four Candles lighting on Christmas Eve and we've kept Mark's favorite restaurants in circulation on his birthday. I don't ever want these remembrances and meaning-making methods to feel like a burden to them. For Milo's 13th birthday, they asked for an amp to learn Mark's electric guitar. I had custom guitar picks made on Etsy with pictures of Mark and Milo when young. Milo loved the gift and felt connected to their dad even though he has been gone for half of their life now.

6. **Support your children's spiritual life.** It was Dr. Julie Kaplow who reminded me in our interview that most kids actually have very active spiritual lives and thoughts of the afterlife can become consuming at times after a loss. Let your kids know you want to hear about their thoughts and feelings on the afterlife and other aspects of their spiritual growth. Acknowledge the unknown and honor the power of that. They need to hear that you are open to all their feelings and needs. If religious affiliation isn't something you are into but they are curious, help them explore in safe ways. Read books together about different faiths. Ask a friend or family member to take them to a service. Inquire about their internal life.

7. **Advocate for your kids at school and with family and friends.** Daddies and Donuts Day? Nope, not for us! It's okay to protect your children from other people's lack of understanding. Soften the blows, even if you have to absorb the pain yourself. No one can understand what your family is going through if they haven't been through it themselves, even the people who may have been supportive in the beginning. The rest of the world has moved on from the giant hole that you all have had to live with for all these years and more to come.

8. **Celebrate the good. Model joy. Honor your growth.** Recovering your life after grief is not only about allowing yourself or your kids to feel positive emotions again but it's also about wanting to model for your kids that yes, while our grief can tear us down and destroy us, the legacy of parental death is not the theft of our lives or of our joy. We all deserve praise for still standing. Like Wanda, we have to honor our pain and find the love within ourselves to persevere. I wanted my children to know they were worthy of love and of joy. So, when Grace is on stage, I bring her all the flowers. And when Milo came out, we celebrated with one big, socially distanced, and masked gay pride pool party with their friends. Life after loss is never only about the loss. It's about learning to live again. It's about leaning into the discomfort and the absence and honoring it, not necessarily filling it. This is our homecoming.

FIFTEEN

The Treasure at the Bottom of the Shipwreck

After about a year of pandemic living, Brian, the kids, and I had all adapted to it pretty well. Both of the kids had restarted therapy and both of them were able to end it again in just a few months, knowing it could be a touchstone when life got hard. After they stopped going, I had the financial opening I needed to return to my own therapy. While Alice seemed to think I was fine, I didn't feel fine. I continued to struggle with my anxiety as we moved into year two in the *after COVID times*. When Grace ended her last go-around of therapy with Elizabeth Davis, I asked Elizabeth for a referral for a therapist for me, one who specialized in complex PTSD. That's how I met Jessica.

During our first session, I told Jessica that I wanted to do some brief therapy to process the events that led up to mine and Brian's wedding, so that the next time I faced overwhelming anxiety, I would cope with it better. Jessica told me that right off the bat, there were two things I needed to know about her: 1. She swore like a sailor and 2. She was a huge geek and fangirl for all things Wonder Woman and Star Wars. I told her we'd get along perfectly.

As Jessica listened to me detail the events of my life in that first session, we made note of all the "big T" (traumatic events involving violence or loss) and "little t" (related or other acutely distressing events) traumas I had endured, starting from age four. It became obvious to Jessica, at least, that my "brief" therapy was going to be more than just a few sessions. I maintained I didn't need to go too deeply, recounting to Jessica all of the other therapy I had done over the years. I shared the good, bad, and in-between therapy I had gone through. I noted my upset that all of my past therapists seemed to agree that I was not particularly good at feeling my feelings. Jessica then asked about the first time I was in therapy with Alice, and if we had processed the totality of the years between my miscarriage in 2010 and Mark's death in 2014. I told her that Alice rolled right from one crisis to another with me. Jessica just nodded her head and said, "Yah-huh."

I told her my biggest goal was to figure out how to get out of my own way. To stop trying to sabotage my happiness now. I wanted to stay healed.

"Okie dokie," she said. She turned to me quite seriously then. "You've lived through a lot of trauma, kid," she said.

"You said Mark's death was the icing on the grief cake. Um, no. Mark's death was the top layer of the seven-layer craptastic casserole and that the only thing to do, frankly, is eat that crap and shit it out. And I know the therapist in you knows all about it, so tell me exactly how that is going to work without going back and connecting not just the dots from the losses in your thirties to your fears now, but all the way back. To the beginning. To the abuse you suffered as a child that started your anxiety and feelings of abandonment." I sighed. It was craptastic. I knew then that this round of therapy was going to be long, hard, and expensive. But Jessica got me. I trusted her immediately. So, we started digging through the shitty casserole together.

In my external life, I am a caretaker. I try to be there to help my loved ones, in particular my children. I have always worked in my career to try to advance justice in solidarity with those who have been denied it by this world. But in my internal life, I have not really let myself stop, for any significant period of time, and hold the weight of HOW much suffering I've gone through. Somehow, it's always felt like I wasn't deserving of acknowledging the hurt or holding the full weight of the losses. I also realized that while I was grieving each individual loss of the last decade, I just kept pushing through them, and before that, through my childhood and adolescence, trying to get to stability. I didn't let myself go deeply into the feelings because I was afraid they would paralyze me. *An object in motion has to stay in motion...*

The emotional work I did in what turned out to be eighteen months of therapy with Jessica was the hardest in my life. We tried EMDR again at the beginning, but I dissociated too quickly when trying to process my abuse. After realizing this, we changed course and began "parts of self" therapy, which is a way to look at your own internal dynamics based on traditional family systems therapy. I told Jessica all about Debbie Ford's books and what I thought of my Shadow. We gave names and ages to the parts of myself that had the big T traumas happen to them. She asked me to visualize all of these parts meeting in a garden. And the wisest part of me, the part that had delivered me right to where I needed to be, to sit with them all and hold their pain.

"What is the myth that you tell yourself?" she asked me to ask the Wise Woman part.

"That I deserve the bad things that have happened to me. Look at all that has happened," I lamented.

"What else?" she said.

"And that if I reach for the thing that makes me happy, if I allow myself to experience joy, then surely, I will bring about the catastrophe that will follow. I never get to be truly happy. It's always stolen from me."

She joked, "Wow! You are really powerful, aren't you? All the ways you control the universe!"

In the child welfare field, we talk about the invisible suitcase that children who suffer abuse and neglect carry. In the suitcase are the thoughts, beliefs, and feelings we all carry forward from our childhood into our adulthood. Some of us also have adult traumas that get added to our suitcases. These experiences shape us the most and are often the places we are most wounded. Jessica and I unpacked each piece of me stuffed into that suitcase that carried these difficult traumas and beliefs, and then we repacked my suitcase with affirmations, with self-love and self-care, and with allowance to grieve and grieve deeply. I grieved my past; that was like a puzzle missing some of its pieces and never quite complete. I grieved for the future I didn't get to have with Mark. And I grieved the present and all the ways I was forced to just keep going, stuffing my feelings down, down, down until the suitcase was ready to burst. We gave my body permission to stop holding it all in.

Jessica and I worked intensively together, all the way until it was time for Brian and myself to finally have our "sequel" wedding in August of 2021. Brian and I had been married fourteen months by the time we were able to have the wedding we originally planned. We had canceled three wedding dates during that time due to the pandemic. I've come to believe that what was meant to be, was. The time in between gave us what we needed to deepen our bond. I joked that if we could survive the first year of marriage together in the house 24/7, we'd be just fine for the rest of our days.

I saw this wedding, the one we wanted to have that COVID robbed us of, as not just a chance to celebrate mine and Brian's love for each other, but to celebrate the ways in which he and I have survived. To celebrate the love from our friends and family that pulled each of us through to become the people we are today. To celebrate ourselves for taking such a risk and loving again despite having known great loss.

When our big day finally came and I arrived at our venue, I was anxious. Why, I don't know, because we were already married and unlike every other major transition in our life, there was no drama the night before. Just a little drama the morning of, when we learned that Brian's mother had a mild fever and decided it best, out of an abundance of caution, to stay home, in case it was COVID. *Adapt*, I told myself. *It is okay. Breathe and push, and don't assume the worst will happen.*

When I went into the venue to touch up my makeup, the event coordinator found me and introduced me to another staff member who would accompany me to meet my needs throughout the day. She introduced herself as Gwyn and it took me a few minutes of side-eyeing her to recognize her. This happened at the same moment she recognized me. It had been twenty years, but I knew Sofia had sent her to me that day. Gwyn had been Sofia's other teenage best friend, and we hadn't seen each other since Sofia's wedding day.

"Did you know she passed away?" she asked me gently, not wanting to ruin my makeup with fresh tears. I led her over to the cake table and showed her where we had created a small display of our loved ones on the other side. Gwyn hadn't known Mark had died either. I quickly filled her in on our story and how Brian and I were finally getting our long-awaited wedding day.

"I'm glad you are here," I told her.

Gwyn walked us out to prepare for my walk down the aisle, through the peony garden at Frank Lloyd Wright's historic Martin House. Milo looped their arm in mine as Grace sang us down the aisle to "Here Comes the Sun," meeting Milo and I half-way, to walk the rest of the way together to Brian. Our minister, Reverend Michelle, this time in person, started by reminding us that even in our darkest hour, God had not abandoned us. Brian and I found love where and when we least expected it. We included prayers for Leah (Brian's late wife) and my mother in our ceremony, along with their rosaries next to the chalice we lit that held their symbolic light. During the meditation, we distributed yellow roses to each of the people who had taken care of us during our darkest days. We took the time to look in their eyes and thank them for all they had done. We cried together. Then, we presented the children with necklaces made from the jewels that Mark had given me, the survivors of the split wedding bands that had to be cut from my hand after he died. Brian and I told Grace and Milo that Mark's love for me would always live on in our love for them. Together, the four of us planted a tree seedling that now grows in our front yard. As we blended soil and water, I let the light of that perfect day fill my heart and remind me that wherever I was, Mark was with me. In the darkest moments and in the brightest. Our imperfect love hadn't died with him. It had only expanded to be universal and all-encompassing.

A week later, when I walked into my scheduled therapy session with Jessica, I had a visitor's sticker from the hospital on my shirt.

"What is that? Oh my god. What happened? Please tell me there was not a catastrophe as you predicted at your wedding!"

I sat down and told her how glorious the wedding day was. And then I told her how the next day, while Brian and I were out kayaking and enjoying our staycation in the city, my father had a heart attack at my house, in front of Grace and Milo. Thankfully, my father's girlfriend, Marilyn (herself a widow and a former nurse) recognized his symptoms and called an ambulance in spite of my father telling her it was just a bad case of indigestion. I am 100% convinced that, alongside Marilyn, my mother was my father's guardian angel that day. It turned out that the nearest hospital emergency room was just closed that hour, having reached full capacity due to a COVID increase. As such, the ambulance carrying my father was forced to turn around and head instead for downtown Buffalo, where the region's vascular institute was. While we waited for hours in the parking lot there (due to COVID protocols), the top cardiologist in the city shocked my father back to life and then cleared the complete blockage in his main artery. I told Jessica I had to go right back to the hospital after our session, but I came because I knew I needed to debrief and to feel the feelings while this latest crisis was happening.

Jessica let out a long sigh and reached under her desk, hauling out a reusable bag with Wonder Woman on it.

"You know, I didn't want to believe you… this belief of yours that bad things always happen when you have good things in your life. But fuck it, maybe you're right. So, this stops now. Let's break the curse." And she started pulling out Florida water, black pepper, bay leaves, rose water, and candles from the bag.

"What is this?" I asked, astounded.

"What does it look like? It's witchcraft," she said matter-of-factly. "The western way isn't working so it's time for the big guns. I've been watching Witch Tok. I'm ready when you are."

I giggled so hard I couldn't stop. Jessica was not amused. This is why I love Jessica. She has never once questioned my spiritualist leanings and if anything, she's been right there encouraging them. She was always prepared to shift gears. I told her I wasn't ready yet to start casting spells, as I had some very specific work I wanted to do first.

"Well, I guess you know yourself best. Seems my therapy is working after all," she said begrudgingly as she pushed the Wonder Woman bag back under the desk.

"Don't worry," I said. "We're getting there."

"You know..." she said a few sessions later, "It wasn't a total catastrophe this time. Your dad lived. Could have been worse. He could have had the heart attack and died at the wedding."

"You are not wrong," I said, as I handed her the candles and herbs I had bought on a trip earlier in the year when I was in Salem, Massachusetts. I wanted her to add them to the magic Wonder Woman bag. Doom and gloom and superstition had been part of my mythology of self for so long, but it was time to wish it all away and replace it with good thoughts and better beliefs about myself. To really do this, I knew I had to make the space in my life to finish out our therapy with more intention, so I started seeing Jessica in two and then three-hour chunks of time. We'd pull out the Wonder Woman witch bag and process what was left to let go of the doom gloom. We poured salt to the earth in remembrance of all the relationships that brought me love and pain; we lit incense to honor all of the losses and to ask the air to support my breath; we lit candles and watched the flames chase away my fears of abandonment as I forgave the parts of myself and the people whose rejection had hurt me the most. Before we ended, Jessica and I also did two, two-day intensive retreats.

On one of our last full days together, a whole year after the sequel wedding, Jessica suggested we go to the beach at the camp where Mark and Sofia and I had all been together in our youth; before I was a mother to my children and before I had to mother my own mother. While I had gone back to camp once or twice since Mark died, it was incredibly painful for me. Then the camp closed. The property was sold, and I couldn't go back again. That little fact didn't matter to Jessica.

"I mean, what are they going to do? Arrest us for trespassing?"

I suggested, instead, that we could go to the public beach next door to the camp and walk up from there.

"I want you to write a eulogy for your friends. I think we need to mourn them there, in that place that is sacred to you and to Mark and Sofia. You need to grieve these losses together." So, it was there, on the shores of Lake Erie, that I gave my grief back to the water.

That morning, sitting in the sand together, I read Jessica the eulogy I had written for the people I had loved and lost. I told the story in the songs that had meant so much to us. I remembered the chosen family I had created at camp and how all the love I had wanted to share was robbed from me due to forces outside of my control. I noticed the sensations in my body that yearned for nurturing when I talked about losing my mother and my baby. I had to grieve all of it, fully and completely. That is why we had come to the water. I had to give myself the compassion I so readily gave to others.

As Jessica collected stones that she would later give me with affirmations written on them to remember our time together, I crossed the boundary onto the camp beach. There was the same giant piece of driftwood we used to sit on and have campfires at night. I was flooded with memories of running down that very beach as teenagers together, laughing with Sofia and in love with Mark. The power of that place had meant so much to us all when we were younger. I let the tears come as I walked into the water. It was a beautiful August day. The sun warmed my body as my feet stepped into the cool, wet sand and the waves lapped at my toes. I took a few more steps into the lake and fell to my knees. I let it all come back to the surface: the agony of their deaths, the hurts and regrets I had harbored, my sadness for losing my unborn baby and my mother, the uncertainty of how the kids and I could survive in this new world we found ourselves tossed into, the joy and fear of falling in love again; the heart broken open.

The tears kept coming and melted into the waves. I waited and expected to be paralyzed. I cried for a while until I noticed the seagulls overhead, pulling my eyes to the blue of the sky. I looked out on the horizon and a calmness settled over me. I was proud of myself for who I had become and who I am still becoming. I knew Mark would be proud of me too. I thought about how sure I had been that I was "over it" when I walked into the ocean in Acadia and, here I was, another four years on and I was again at the water's edge, trying to make sense of it all. I walked back to Jessica, this time knowing that I had actually done the emotional labor to start resolving the pain AND recognizing that it would never be "done" and I would never be "over it."

She handed me a few rocks from the beach.

"Are you ready to make your container to hold your pain now?"

If you've ever done therapy, you've probably heard of the emotional container. It harkens back to the groundbreaking work of Carl Jung (who also first theorized the Shadow self) and has to do with envisioning a container for holding our upsetting thoughts, emotions, and memories when it is not a good time to be aware of them. While it seems counterintuitive, as it is by its nature, a little dissociative, being able to compartmentalize how and when you visit your grief can be adaptive in not having it overwhelm you at all the most inconvenient times. While I've watched emotional containment work well when I've led it in therapy with kids and families and I watched my own children benefit from creating containers together with their therapists, I, of course, had thought it juvenile and wholly unnecessary for myself. But as therapy with Jessica had progressed, I saw the benefit. Therapy itself had acted as an emotional container for me. Jessica was there to bear witness to my pain; to honor it with me as something both within and outside of myself. In the early years after the shipwreck that left me widowed and bereft, I just kept swimming until I reached the shore of what turned out to feel like a deserted island. In the beginning, it was. Until I found the people who got me. And then I threw myself into rebuilding our lives; picking up the pieces of what was left of my former life that had washed on shore and trying to use them to create another vessel to carry my family forward. With Jessica's help, I finished that vessel and now I had set sail back into the past so that I could learn to live again in the present. I realized in the weeks leading up to our trip to the beach, that the container was not just about keeping the memories that sought to overwhelm me from spilling out at the wrong times, but there was something deeper there. I knew there was only one type of container I could build that day.

As Jessica unpacked our go-to ceremonial salt, lavender, crystals, and candles from her Wonder Woman bag, I pulled out a box of craft sticks and a container of beach glass from my bag. As I had done so many hundreds of times as a camp counselor, I set about to make a craft stick box. When the paint and glue had dried, I sang my last song for my friends, the same hymn we sang at the final fire when each week of camp came to a close. I placed the pictures of my loved ones in the box, along with sentimental objects from Mark and Sofia and a medal of St. Anne, to represent my mother. I tasted the salt of my tears as I also wrote out each of my strengths on pieces of beach glass and I tucked them in around the objects I had placed inside the craft stick box that I would think of now as my sunken treasure chest. When I found the courage to not only return to the site of the shipwreck but to dive down deep, deep, deeper than I ever had before to look at my pain, it was then and there that I found gold.

SIXTEEN

A Song from the Sea

All children and all adults want to be loved, to be seen as worthwhile, to be important, and to be capable. These are the components of our self-concept. When we go through trauma and loss, it challenges our self-worth. How quickly we can move—in the time between falling asleep and waking up, or between waiting on results of an MRI and the news that leaves us in shock, or as we watch the police officer approach our front door—from capable to incapable. From being important to someone else to being utterly alone. It has taken me seven, almost eight, years to write this book. I have often felt incapable during this time; like I would never be at a place where I could be whole enough to write it. I've often felt unloved in these years, even though my community, my children, and my significant other loved me deeply. I have felt unimportant, like an imposter who didn't belong at a camp for widowed people. And I have felt useless. I know you have felt these things, too. When I feel my worst, I remember the gold I found that was buried in my sunken treasure chest. Opening it, I remember I have everything I need in me to not only survive Mark's death, but to thrive as I set sail again into the ocean of life.

What is in my treasure chest, you ask? For one, there is now a belief that I truly deserve happiness. And that whatever future troubles come my way, they are circumstantial to who I am. They will no longer define who I am or who I can be. I found a belief that I deserve happiness, joy, peace, calm, and all the good things. I found that I deserve the gift of time to see my children grow up and to, one day, watch my grandchildren playing in my garden. For in the treasure chest, shimmering like gold, was my wisest self, pulling me through the worst moments of my life. I had to learn to surrender my control and trust her. To let go of what I had expected my life to be or look like. She showed me how to be vulnerable. She showed me how to feel pain. She showed me that love never dies. She showed me the magic within that only comes when one is drowning and somehow it is in the chaos that you find within you the power to propel towards the light, towards breath.

This book has taken me almost eight years to write because it's so hard as a solo parent (even after getting an amazing co-parent) to find time alone to invest in creative pursuits. I also recognized that I needed to do the emotional labor to birth these words onto the page. I watched other people's books magically materialize from start to finish during this time and I asked myself why I couldn't get it together enough to finish the book. Jessica wondered if perhaps I was not finishing it, because then it might be time to let the story of my grief subside.

As summer turned into fall this past year, I determined that I couldn't finish this book without getting some more time alone. Jessica and I were preparing to end therapy and I had been thinking hard since our trip to the beach about what I needed to do to keep myself afloat when I didn't have her to rely on. How would I trust that my sunken treasure would be enough to see me through the hard times? Could I really set sail in a ship of my own making and not drown? I went, as I had done a few times before, to an old estate a few hours away, where I rented a suite for a solo writing retreat. As I drove out, I thought a lot about legacy. What was the legacy of my loss that I wanted to impart in this book so that a newly widowed parent reading this would know they could survive the pain they were in? What would be the legacy of the loss of their father for Milo and Grace?

I am so proud of how far Milo and Grace have come from their shipwreck. I know Mark would be proud of them, too. When he first died, my greatest concern was whether I could keep their mental health intact. I am relieved to say that they are doing just fine today. We all have our good days and our bad days but by and large, my children have survived and thrived. Before I left for this writing retreat, Milo and I had a therapy session with their counselor, after a year-long break. Milo has been dealing with fairly regular homophobic bullying at school. The more I've watched my child find their true self and their voice, the more I've watched the world try to silence them. Milo's counselor pulled me aside and said how very proud I should be of my kiddo. She couldn't get over how well Milo was doing, in spite of the struggles at school. Milo didn't even flinch when mentioning casually to her that I was going away for three days, and they'd be home with Brian and Grace. The time away from each other doesn't just serve me. It serves my children too. They learn to rely on each other and their stepfather more. Grace will soon be going off to college. She is planning on becoming a music therapist, combining her art with her gift of endless compassion for those who are hurting.

It wasn't until I was sitting out on the big porch at the retreat center, watching the sun return after a heavy rain, that I let myself think about Mark's legacy. It was only when I took a break from thinking about his legacy and what I wanted to say about it, that the answer came. I went into my room to make a cup of coffee and while it was brewing, I meandered about the space in between my room and the entryway to the porch. It was then that I noticed for the first time a table behind the door. On the table, was a memorial book to mark the lives and legacies of the people who had contributed over the years to the care and upkeep of the retreat center. Next to it, there was a picture frame, with an instruction to add to the book about why you were there. Also included in the frame was an excerpt cut out from *The Little Prince,* which just so happened to be Mark's favorite childhood book. It read:

> *In one of the stars,*
>
> *I shall be living.*
>
> *In one of them,*
>
> *I shall be laughing.*
>
> *And so it will be as if all of the stars*
>
> *were laughing,*
>
> *when you look at the sky at night.*[36]

---

36 An excerpt from Antoine de Saint-Exupery's *The Little Prince* (Clarion Books, 2000) as seen at Cobblestone Springs Retreat Center in Dundee, NY.

Trauma can't be made not traumatic, I whispered, reminding myself that I don't have to see Mark's life or his death as only trauma, pain, and loss. Mark's legacy was not only the beauty of our love grown in my children. It was not the scars he caused me or himself on his worst days. I have come to believe in the most essential law of the universe: energy can neither be created nor destroyed. And as such, Mark, who he was, his essence, his energy, is in the stars now. It is in the soil I dig my hands in. It is in the sun shining on my face after the rain. It is in the chirps of the birds and the breeze on my arms. It's in the ocean of the grief I've carried and in the waters of Lake Erie where I've dived down to find the gold in myself I had long buried.

Mark's legacy is the life our children will lead. It has been gifted forward to all of the people we've tried to help in his name. His story will be told in Milo's guitar chords, in Grace's mezzo soprano, in the words I put down on these written pages and the poems I speak from the mouth he once kissed. He was my first and longest love. For me, losing Mark stripped away all that was non-essential in my psyche and in my relationships to other people. My husband's death made me question everything about my life. Letting myself be honest about who he was, what we gave and took from each other, and allowing myself to deeply grieve him while acknowledging the weight of the other losses in my life, transformed who I was. It brought into sharp focus who I made time for now, how I parented now, and what I wanted to do with the one wild and precious life given to me.

In the years that have followed his death, I've changed my address (three times now), my career, my friends, and the way I am as a mother, as a lover, and as a human being. I've gotten comfortable being alone and in my own skin. I've found my worth and my importance. I know I am loved. And I know death is but a shadow. His spirit lives. Everywhere I go, when I look for him, he is there.

If I have final words to impart about your life after loss, it's this. **Don't let their death define your life.** You can honor your lost partner. You can mourn the hell out of it. You can visit the shipwreck whenever you need to. Swim down to the depths of the ocean and think about letting the weight of it wash you away if you need to. But you can also fight to swim to the surface. Get to the light and summon the courage to swim to shore, even though you are tired.

And when you get to shore, rest. Rebuild. Rest some more. And at some point, the tide will turn, and the water will start to gently lap at your toes again, beckoning you back into the ocean. Fight the urge to stay in the safety of your island. Answer the ocean's call. Chart your course and get back out there. Don't let the undertows catch you off guard. Remain calm. Sail off into the sunset, even knowing — especially knowing—that there will be other storms that you will suffer but you know now that have an unshakeable strength to survive. Live your life amongst the waves and sunshine. Live it to the fullest. Look up to the stars at night to guide you on your journeys. Pass your fierce love of life onto your children who will pass it onto their children. And let their wholeness be your shared legacy.

THE END

ACKNOWLEDGEMENTS

I would like to first offer thanks to my children, Grace and Milo Koncikowski, whose love and lives are the very reason I found the strength to get us to shore. Their unconditional support from the start of "the book" has put the wind in the sails of this writing project. I thank them especially for not only letting me tell their stories but to trust me wholly with them. They are beautiful, fierce, and incredibly kind children. Their father would be so proud of them.

Thank you to my brothers, John and Michael, and my father, Dennis. Mike, I think you missed a spot painting my hallway! Seriously though, thank you for standing by and looking out for the kids and I at every turn. Johnny, thank you for coming up immediately and helping me through the hardest days. Dad, you gave me permission to live my life in the "after" in the way I wanted to. Thank you for all the ways you stepped in as a caregiver, so I didn't have to fly solo 24/7 the first few years.

I am indebted to the group of women who lifted me up from the first hours in the after. Thank you to Stephanie, Olive, and Stacy for dropping everything to get to us and staying with us for the first week. Having you by our sides got us through the wake and the burial. A special shoutout to Haley and Steph as well for always looking out for my children: in the past, in the present, and in the future. Your steadfast friendship has meant the world to me. I love you both.

Thank you also to my cousin, Beth, for crossing the country to be with me after everyone else had to return to their lives and bringing the silliness we needed when everything was so damn serious. I am also grateful for the ways my cousins Cheryl, Mark, and Amanda, cared for our family.

All of my appreciation to Amy and Matt, mine, and Mark's dearest friends, who we had spent so much of our lives with. Thank you for all the ways you have continued to care for me and the kids in the years since we lost him. I am also indebted to Andrea and Chris for making me leave the house the first year and giving the kids an outing at every holiday. Thanks also to Amy F. and Bridget for their regular mental health check-ins as well as to Beth, Barnaby, and Joe for the ways they supported my mental and physical health.

I have deep love and affection for mine and Mark's "second wife,"Erin. E, I really don't know how I could have gotten through these years without you by my side. I know Mark would be so incredibly appreciative of the ways in which you went from loving him to loving me. You were often the only one who could get the kids and I giggling on the darkest days. Thank you for listening to my drama at countless coffee shops over the last eight years, for sharing in my "miracle at Lily Dale," and for making sure our first Christmas Eve was not spent alone.

I was blessed to meet Erika three weeks after Mark died. Thank you, Erika, for being the stranger that offered me a soft landing and opening your home and heart to me. Your friendship and the generous ways you gave of your time and care when we felt so destroyed early in our grief will never be forgotten. Without you, this story wouldn't be this story. You were my compass.

I am thankful for the love and support of my CDHS family: Joshua, Alisha, and Kristin. To my adopted brother, Josh, thank you for pushing me to write outside of my comfort zone. To my soul sisters, Alisha and Kristin: I have so much gratitude for the two of you! You have both been there for me in so many ways the last eight years. I love you both and thank you for all the kindness you have shown our family. Alisha, we live in the knowing. Kristin, you were the first by my side, you offered your services as a minister to lay Mark to rest, and you so generously spent hours and hours helping me craft this story. Thank you for being my editor, my friend, and my stand-in mother. The clarity you helped me find strengthened our story.

When I set out on this writing project, I knew I wanted to tell more than my family's story. Thank you to the following widowed parents for baring their souls and sharing their families' stories with me: Emma, Lucy, Arash, Bo, Michele, Bridget, Jessica, David, Pat, Chris, Annmarie, Brandi, Lisa, Matt, Scott, Taya, Holly, Matt, Terri, Bethany, and Morwenna. Taken together, I pray that the lessons in our stories provide a map to help other widowed parents navigate through the deep waters. A special thank you to Rev. Lauren for mentoring me through the murky waters of SUDEP and throwing me another life preserver when I needed it. I send immense love and appreciation out to the universe for the life of my friend, Luke. Luke, I want you to know that your legacy and love live on. Thank you for asking me to include your story here.

I also have deep gratitude for the clinicians and scholars who shared their work and stories with me. Thank you to Dr. Julie Kaplow and Dr. Jill Harrington, who I had the privilege of working with during my time as a consultant with the National Child Traumatic Stress Network. Your new theories on grief are going to be so helpful for parents to consider as they look for new ways to support their children's mental health. Thanks also to Chris who introduced me to NCTSN and has always encouraged me forward.

A very special thank you to Elizabeth Davis, Kate, Melissa, and Alice who have provided my children and I with excellent mental health care. Without the four of you, I'm not sure we'd be as well as we are today. Thank you for bearing witness to our pain.

Blessings in my life came from meeting Emily, Gerldine, and Nicole. Emily, thank you for providing the space for our family to mourn together, for holding space with me and my children in community, and for trusting me to advocate on behalf of others who have a shared experience. I am grateful for all the ways we have worked together over the years. Gerldine, you have mentored me through my growth as a leader, as a caregiver, and as a community activist. Thank you for standing on sacred ground with me and always answering my every offer and opportunity to work together with a solid, "Yes!" I appreciate the ways you've made me think about equity in grief, in service provision, and whose stories we tell and hear. You move mountains and I am thankful to call you a friend. Nicole, you arrived in my life as a student and now you are teaching me a thing or two about semicolon usage, among other important lessons. I am deeply grateful that you were willing to act as a developmental editor on a later version of this book. Additionally, without the power of these three women and I together, Grassroots Gardens WNY's Gardening Through Grief program would not have been spoken into being. Big thanks also to my staff and board at GGWNY for their trust in me.

The award for the most BAMF therapist out there goes to Jessica Horder. Thank you, Jessica, for gently pushing me towards rumbling with the real grief under the seen grief. My parts and I are forever indebted to the lessons we learned together. You truly went above and beyond for me.

Sofia, you are never far from my mind or heart. When we meet again, we will have so much to catch up on, sitting there together on the porch of our favorite cabin. S.W.A.K.

Brian Bingeman, you are my love of *this* life. Your love has restored my faith, it has guided my ship home, and it has created space for my true self to emerge from the waters. It's really not that complicated.

To my beloved Mark, I pray that wherever you are now, you are happy. I wish our time together could have been longer. I wish we could have seen what our repair looked like. I am so proud of all you did at the end to grow. I know that if you could, you would tell me to write it as it was, which is what I've done. Thank you for leaving me your words, your poems, and your books. I take great comfort in them. Whenever I look at our children, I know you are not gone from us. You are right there in them, shining through Grace's big heart and Milo's smart skepticism. You know what you mean to me, what you've always meant. Your life and your death have shaped me but I know now how to define who I am. Thank you for being the holder of my stories. I love you, always.

ABOUT THE AUTHOR

Jeanette Koncikowski is a writer, activist, community educator, and advocate. Born and raised in Buffalo, NY, Jeanette received her undergraduate degree in Psychology and Women's Studies from the University of Buffalo in 2000 and completed her Master's degree in Education at Harvard University in 2001. She has spent over twenty five years working in the nonprofit field: first as a crisis counselor, then an instructional designer in the child welfare training field, and most recently, she directed a regional community garden organization. In 2023, she launched her own consulting firm, Thrive Community Consulting LLC, to continue to support community health.

Since the death of her first husband in 2014, Jeanette has supported other widowed parents in navigating their way forward. She launched the Widowed Parent Project in 2016 (as both a Facebook support page and a Twitter-based resource feed: @widowedpp). She has since worked with the National Child Traumatic Stress Network to create an educational resource series of handouts for grieving parents entitled *The Power of Parenting*. She has been a featured guest on several podcasts and blogs about parenting through grief. She also offers coaching to widowed people. You can learn more about her work at thrivecommunityconsulting.com.

When not detailing the tragedies and triumphs of her life in memoir, you can find her at peace in her garden, with her two thriving children, her husband, Brian, and two rescued pups by her side.